Classroom Treats

Table of Contents

Classroom Treats

Giant Gift Boxes

1 package (18¼ ounces) chocolate or vanilla cake mix, plus ingredients to prepare mix
1 container (16 ounces) white frosting
Green and orange food coloring
Yellow decorating icing
Candy sprinkles
Candles (optional)

1. Prepare and bake cake mix according to package directions for two 8- or 9-inch square cakes. Cool completely before frosting.

2. Blend half of frosting and green food coloring in medium bowl until desired shade is reached. Repeat with remaining frosting and orange food coloring.

3. Place one cake layer on serving plate; frost top and sides with green frosting. Pipe stripe of yellow icing on each side to resemble ribbon. Let frosting set before adding second cake layer. Place second cake layer slightly off-center and rotated 45 degrees from bottom layer as shown in photo. Frost top and sides with orange frosting. Pipe stripe of yellow icing on each side to resemble ribbon.

4. Pipe additional yellow icing on top of cake for bow and streamers as shown in photo. Decorate cake with candy sprinkles and candles, if desired.

Makes 12 servings

Candy Bar Cake

1 package (18¼ ounces)
   devil's food cake mix
   without pudding in the
   mix
1 cup sour cream
4 eggs
⅓ cup vegetable oil
¼ cup water
3 containers (16 ounces
   each) white frosting
1 bar (2.1 ounces)
   chocolate-covered
   crispy peanut butter
   candy, chopped
1 bar (2.07 ounces)
   chocolate-covered
   peanut, caramel and
   nougat candy, chopped
1 bar (1.4 ounces)
   chocolate-covered
   toffee candy, chopped
4 bars (1.55 ounces each)
   milk chocolate

1. Preheat oven to 350°F. Grease and flour two 9-inch round cake pans.

2. Beat cake mix, sour cream, eggs, oil and water in large bowl with electric mixer at low speed about 1 minute or until blended. Increase speed to medium; beat 1 to 2 minutes or until smooth. Spread batter in prepared pans.

3. Bake 30 to 35 minutes or until toothpick inserted into centers comes out clean. Cool in pans on wire racks 10 minutes; remove from pans and cool completely on wire racks.

4. Cut each cake layer in half horizontally. Place one cake layer on serving plate. Spread generously with one fourth of frosting. Sprinkle with one chopped candy bar. Repeat with two more cake layers, additional frosting and remaining two chopped candy bars. Top with remaining cake layer; frost top of cake with remaining frosting.

5. Break milk chocolate bars into pieces along score lines. Stand chocolate pieces in frosting around outside edge of cake as shown in photo.

Makes 12 servings

Happy Birthday Cookies

½ cup (1 stick) butter,
    softened
⅓ cup granulated sugar
⅓ cup packed brown sugar
 1 egg
½ teaspoon vanilla
1¼ cups flour
½ teaspoon baking powder
¼ teaspoon baking soda
¼ teaspoon salt
¾ cup mini candy-coated
    chocolate pieces
½ cup chocolate-covered
    toffee chips
½ cup peanut butter and
    milk chocolate chips
½ cup lightly salted peanuts,
    coarsely chopped

1. Preheat oven to 375°F. Line cookie sheets with parchment paper.

2. Beat butter and sugars in large bowl with electric mixer at medium speed until fluffy. Beat in egg and vanilla. Combine flour, baking powder, baking soda and salt in large bowl. Add to butter mixture; stir until well blended. Stir in chocolate pieces, chips and peanuts until well blended.

3. Drop dough by rounded tablespoonfuls 2 inches apart onto prepared cookie sheets. Bake 10 minutes or until firm and golden brown. Let cookies stand 1 minute. Remove to wire racks; cool completely.

Makes 3 dozen cookies

Cubcakes

 1 package (18¼ ounces)
    chocolate cake mix,
    plus ingredients to
    prepare mix
 1 container (16 ounces)
    chocolate frosting
 1 package (5 ounces)
    chocolate nonpareil
    candies
72 red cinnamon candies
    Chocolate sprinkles
    Black decorating gel

1. Line 24 standard (2½-inch) muffin cups with paper baking cups or spray with nonstick cooking spray.

2. Prepare cake mix and bake in prepared pans according to package directions. Cool cupcakes in pans on wire racks 15 minutes. Remove cupcakes to wire racks; cool completely.

3. Frost cooled cupcakes with chocolate frosting. Use nonpareils to create ears and muzzle. Add cinnamon candies for eyes and noses. Decorate with chocolate sprinkles for fur. Use decorating gel to place dots on eyes and create mouth.

Makes 24 cupcakes

Birthday Cake Cookies

1 package (18 ounces)
   refrigerated sugar
   cookie dough
1 container (16 ounces)
   prepared white frosting
Food coloring (optional)
Colored sprinkles or
   decors
10 small birthday candles

1. Preheat oven to 350°F. Lightly grease 10 mini (1¾-inch) muffin cups and 10 standard (2½-inch) muffin cups. Shape one third of dough into 10 (1-inch) balls; press onto bottoms and up sides of prepared mini muffin cups. Shape remaining two thirds of dough into 10 equal balls; press onto bottoms and up sides of prepared standard muffin cups.

2. Bake mini cookies 8 to 9 minutes or until edges are light brown. Bake regular cookies 10 to 11 minutes or until edges are light brown. Cool 5 minutes in pans on wire racks. Remove cookies to wire racks; cool completely.

3. Add food coloring, if desired, to frosting; mix well. Spread frosting over top and side of each cookie. Place 1 mini cookie on top of 1 regular cookie. Decorate with sprinkles. Press 1 candle into center of each cookie. *Makes 10 cookie cakes*

•super suggestion

These delightful cookies would also taste great using chocolate chip or peanut butter cookie dough in place of the sugar cookie dough.

Happy Happy Birthday .ϑ.

Happy Clown Face

1. Prepare and bake cake mix according to package directions for two 8- or 9-inch round cakes. Cool cake layers completely before frosting.

2. Combine frosting and food coloring in medium bowl until desired shade is reached. Place one cake layer on serving plate; spread with frosting. Top with second cake layer; frost top and side of cake.

3. Decorate face of clown using assorted candies. Arrange party hat and candles on cake as desired.

Makes 12 servings

1 package (18¼ ounces)
    white cake mix, plus
    ingredients to prepare
    mix
1 container (16 ounces)
    white frosting
    Food coloring
    Assorted gum drops,
      gummy candies,
      colored licorice strings
      and other candies
1 party hat
    Candles

Lazy Daisy Cupcakes

1. Line 24 standard (2½-inch) muffin cups with paper baking cups or spray with nonstick cooking spray. Prepare and bake cake mix in prepared muffin cups according to package directions. Cool in pans on wire racks 15 minutes. Remove cupcakes to racks; cool completely.

2. Add food coloring to frosting, a few drops at a time, until desired shade is reached. Frost cooled cupcakes with tinted frosting.

3. Cut each marshmallow crosswise into 4 pieces with scissors. Stretch pieces into petal shapes; place 5 pieces on each cupcake to form flower. Place candy in center of each flower.

Makes 24 cupcakes

1 package (18¼ ounces)
    yellow cake mix, plus
    ingredients to prepare
    mix
    Yellow food coloring
1 container (16 ounces)
    vanilla frosting
30 marshmallows
24 small round candies or
    gumdrops

HAPPY CLOWN FACE

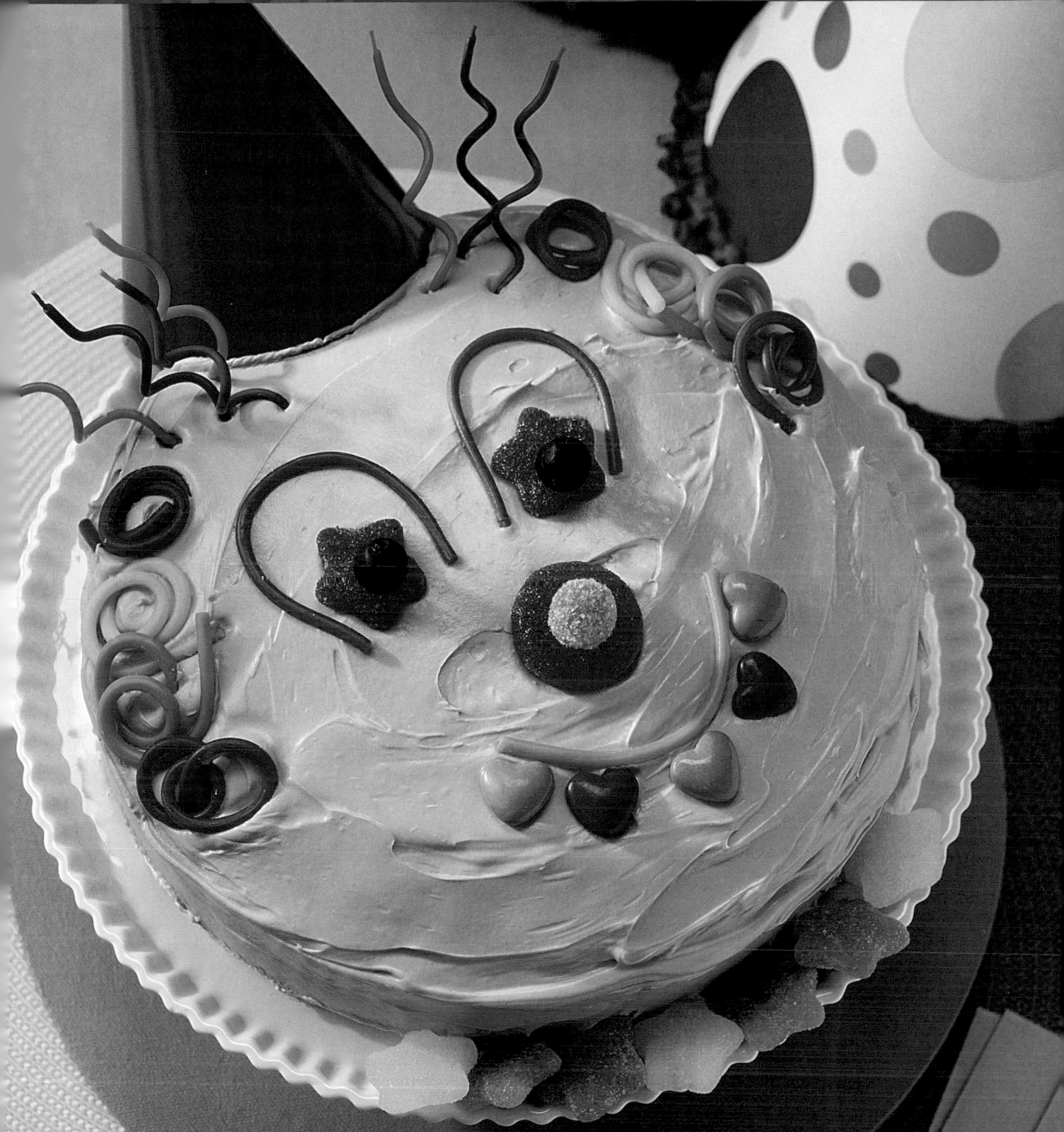

Colossal Birthday Cupcake

1 package (18¼ ounces)
    devil's food cake mix,
    plus ingredients to
    prepare mix
1 container (16 ounces)
    vanilla or chocolate
    frosting, divided
¼ cup peanut butter
    Construction paper or
    aluminum foil
    Fruit-flavored candy
    wafers or chocolate
    shavings
    Candle (optional)

1. Preheat oven to 350°F. Grease and flour two 8-inch round cake pans.

2. Prepare cake mix according to package directions. Pour into prepared pans. Bake about 30 minutes or until toothpick inserted into centers comes out clean. Cool completely before frosting.

3. Blend ¾ cup frosting and peanut butter in medium bowl. Place one cake layer on serving plate; spread frosting mixture evenly over cake layer. Top with second cake layer; frost top with remaining frosting, mounding frosting slightly higher in center.

4. Cut 36×3½-inch piece of construction paper; pleat paper every ½ inch. Wrap around side of cake to resemble baking cup. Arrange candy wafers decoratively on frosting. Place candle in center of cake, if desired.

Makes 12 servings

•super suggestion

Make sure the cake is completely cool before frosting it. Brush off any loose crumbs from the cake's surface. To keep the cake plate clean, place small pieces of waxed paper under the edges of the cake; remove them after the cake has been frosted. For best results, use a flat metal spatula for applying frosting. You will achieve a more professional look if you first apply a thin layer of frosting on the cake as a base coat to help seal in any remaining crumbs. Refrigerate 10 to 15 minutes to set frosting before applying final coat.

Movie Marquee

1 package (18¼ ounces) chocolate cake mix, plus ingredients to prepare mix
1 container (16 ounces) white frosting
1 bag (13 ounces) chocolate candy kisses
Happy Birthday candles or decorating frosting
Star-shaped gummy candies
Star-shaped candies

1. Prepare and bake cake mix according to package directions for 13×9-inch cake. Cool cake completely in pan on wire rack.

2. Frost top of cake. Arrange candy kisses around border of cake. Decorate as desired with candles and candies.   *Makes 12 servings*

Surprise Package Cupcakes

1 package (18¼ ounces) chocolate cake mix, plus ingredients to prepare mix
Food coloring (optional)
1 container (16 ounces) vanilla frosting
1 tube (4¼ ounces) white decorator icing
72 chewy fruit squares
Colored decors and birthday candles (optional)

1. Line 24 standard (2½-inch) muffin cups with paper baking cups or spray with nonstick cooking spray. Prepare and bake cake mix in prepared muffin cups according to package directions. Cool in pans on wire racks 15 minutes. Remove cupcakes to racks; cool completely.

2. If desired, tint frosting with food coloring, adding a few drops at a time until desired color is reached. Spread frosting over cupcakes.

3. Use decorator icing to pipe "ribbons" on fruit squares to resemble wrapped presents. Place 3 candy "presents" on each cupcake. Decorate with decors and candles, if desired.

Makes 24 cupcakes

Spooky S'mores

40 mini marshmallows
40 wonton skins
20 small animal crackers or graham cracker cookies
¹⁄₃ cup chocolate chunks
6 tablespoons plus 2 teaspoons raspberry jam
1 egg, beaten
Canola oil
Powdered sugar

1. Freeze mini marshmallows for at least 1 hour.

2. Place 20 wonton skins on counter. Keep remainder covered with damp cloth. Place 1 cracker in center of each wonton. Top with 2 frozen mini marshmallows, 2 chocolate chunks and 1 teaspoon raspberry jam.

3. Working with one prepared wonton at a time, brush edges of wonton skin with beaten egg. Top with reserved wonton, pressing edges to seal. Gently fold or crimp wonton to curl up edges. Repeat with remaining prepared and reserved wonton skins. Cover with plastic wrap until ready to cook.

4. Fill large, deep skillet with 2 inches oil. Place over medium-high heat. Heat oil to 350°F. Line baking sheet with paper towels. Gently place 2 to 3 s'mores into hot oil. Do not crowd or let edges touch. Cook 2 minutes per side or until golden.

5. Remove s'mores with slotted spoon to prepared baking sheet. Sprinkle powdered sugar over hot s'mores. Let cool 5 minutes before serving.

Makes 20 s'mores

Candy Corn by the Slice

1 package (13.8 ounces) refrigerated pizza crust dough
½ cup shredded mozzarella cheese
2 cups (8 ounces) shredded Cheddar cheese, divided
⅓ cup pizza sauce

1. Preheat oven to 400°F. Spray 13-inch round pizza pan with nonstick cooking spray. Fit pizza dough into pan, shaping as needed.

2. Sprinkle mozzarella in 4-inch circle in center of pizza dough. Sprinkle 1 cup Cheddar cheese in 3-inch ring around center circle. Spoon pizza sauce over Cheddar cheese. Create 1½-inch border around edge of pizza with remaining 1 cup Cheddar cheese.

3. Bake 12 to 15 minutes or until edge is lightly browned and cheese is melted and bubbling. Cut into wedges. *Makes 8 slices*

Green Meanies

4 green apples
1 cup nut butter (cashew, almond or peanut butter)
Almond slivers

1. Place apple, stem side up, on cutting board. Cut away 2 halves from sides of apple, leaving 1-inch-thick center slice with stem and core. Discard core slice. Cut each half round in half. Then cut each apple quarter into two wedges using a crinkle cutter. Each apple will yield 8 wedges.

2. Spread 2 teaspoons nut butter on wide edge of apple slice. Top with another crinkled edge apple slice, aligning crinkled edges to resemble jaws. Insert almond slivers to make fangs.

Makes 8 servings

Tip: For best effect, use a crinkle cutter garnishing tool to create a toothy look.

Jack-o'-Lantern Chili Cups

2 cans (11.5 ounces each) refrigerated corn breadstick dough (8 breadsticks each) *or* 3 cans (4.5 ounces each) refrigerated buttermilk biscuits (6 biscuits each)
1 can (15 ounces) mild chili with beans
1 cup frozen corn
6 slices Cheddar cheese
  Olive slices, bell pepper and carrot pieces for decoration

1. Preheat oven to 425°F. Lightly grease 16 to 18 standard (2½-inch) muffin cups. Lightly roll out corn breadstick dough to press together perforations. Cut out 16 to 18 circles with 3-inch round cookie cutter. Press 1 circle onto bottom and 1 inch up side of each muffin cup.

2. Combine chili and corn in medium bowl. Fill each muffin cup with 1 tablespoon chili mixture. Cut out 16 to 18 circles from cheese with 2 inch round cookie cutter; place rounds over chili mixture in cups. Decorate cheese with olive slices, bell pepper and carrot pieces to resemble jack-o'-lanterns. Bake 10 to 12 minutes or until corn bread is completely baked and cheese is melted.

Makes about 8 servings

Ghost on a Stick

4 wooden craft sticks
4 medium pears, stems removed
9 squares (2 ounces each) almond bark
  Mini chocolate chips

1. Line baking sheet with waxed paper and 4 paper baking cups. Insert wooden sticks into stem ends of pears.

2. Melt almond bark according to package directions.

3. Dip one pear into melted almond bark, spooning bark over top to coat evenly. Remove excess by scraping pear bottom across rim of measuring cup. Place on paper baking cup; let set 1 minute.

4. Decorate with mini chocolate chips to make ghost face. Repeat with remaining pears. Place spoonful of extra almond bark at bottom of pears for ghost tails. Refrigerate until firm.

Makes 4 servings

JACK-O'-LANTERN CHILI CUPS

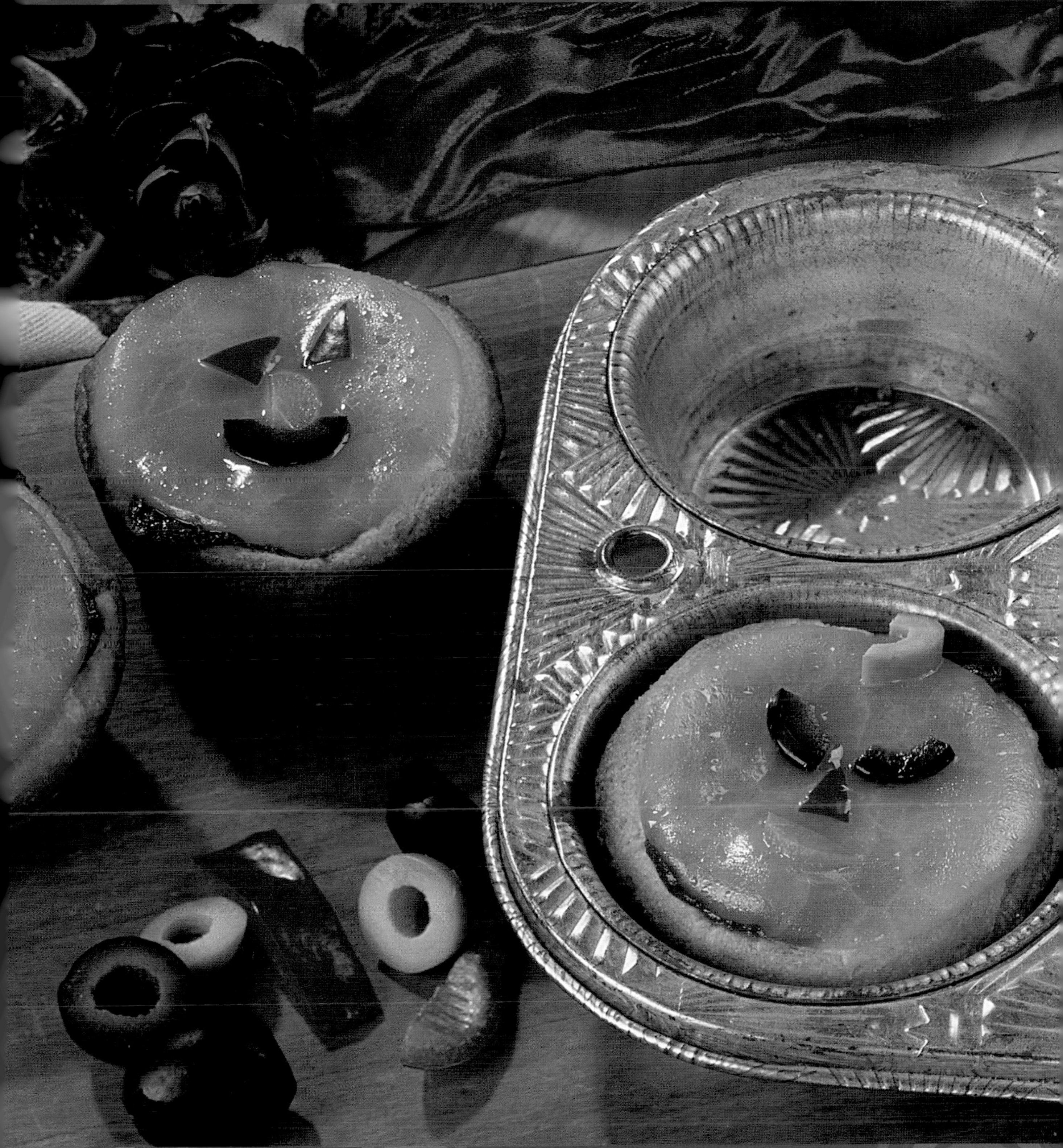

Merlin's Magic Mix

6 cups unbuttered popped
   popcorn, lightly salted
1 cup pretzel nuggets
1 cup slivered almonds,
   toasted and lightly
   salted
¼ cup (½ stick) butter
¼ cup light corn syrup
¾ cup packed light brown
   sugar
⅓ cup red cinnamon
   candies
1 cup mini candy-coated
   chocolate pieces
¾ cup sweetened dried
   cranberries

1. Preheat oven to 250°F. Place popped popcorn in large bowl. Add pretzel nuggets and almonds; set aside. Lightly grease 2 large baking pans; set aside.

2. Combine butter and corn syrup in medium saucepan. Heat over low heat until melted; stir in brown sugar. Cook, stirring constantly, until sugar is melted and mixture comes to a boil. Boil mixture 5 minutes, stirring often. Remove from heat and add cinnamon candies, stirring until melted.

3. Stir sugar mixture into popcorn mixture with lightly greased spatula until evenly coated. Spread popcorn mixture in even layer in prepared pans. Bake 10 to 15 minutes, stirring every 5 minutes with lightly greased spoon to separate popcorn. Cool completely in pans on wire racks.

4. Combine popcorn mixture, candy pieces and cranberries in large bowl. Store in tightly covered container.

Makes about 8 cups

super suggestion

Try substituting your child's favorite nuts for almonds and peanut- or peanut butter-filled candy coated chocolate pieces for mini pieces.

Candy Corn Crispie Treats

½ cup (1 stick) butter or margarine
9 cups mini marshmallows
10 cups chocolate crispy rice cereal
2 cups candy corn
¾ cup mini chocolate chips
Assorted candy pumpkins

1. Melt butter in large saucepan over medium heat. Add marshmallows and stir until smooth.

2. Pour cereal, candy corn and chocolate chips into large bowl. Pour marshmallow mixture over cereal mixture, stirring quickly to coat. For best results, use a wooden spoon sprayed with nonstick cooking spray.

3. Spread mixture on large buttered jelly-roll pan, pressing out evenly with buttered hands. While still warm, press on candy pumpkins spaced about 1½ inches apart.

4. Cool; cut into squares.

Makes about 48 squares

Bloody Monster Claws

5 small red potatoes, scrubbed and cut into 4 slices lengthwise, about ¼ inch thick
¼ cup extra virgin olive oil
Paprika
Salt and pepper to taste
Variety of ketchups (purple, green or mystery)

1. Preheat oven to 425°F.

2. Cut 2 wedges into end of each potato slice to resemble claw.

3. Place oil in 15×10×1-inch jelly-roll pan; tilt to coat bottom evenly. Place potato slices evenly in prepared pan. Sprinkle slices with paprika; turn to coat with oil and sprinkle with paprika. Bake 5 minutes. Turn slices; bake 4 minutes longer or until just fork tender. Sprinkle with salt and pepper. Serve with ketchups.

Makes 20 claws

Quick Sand

¾ cup creamy peanut butter
5 ounces cream cheese, softened
1 cup pineapple preserves
⅓ cup milk
1 teaspoon Worcestershire sauce
  Dash hot pepper sauce (optional)
1 can (7 ounces) refrigerated breadstick dough (6 breadsticks)
5 rich round crackers, crushed
  Cut-up vegetables such as carrots and celery, or fruit such as apples and pears, for dipping

1. Combine peanut butter and cream cheese in large bowl until well blended. Stir in preserves, milk, Worcestershire sauce and hot pepper sauce, if desired. Transfer to serving bowl or spread in 8- or 9-inch glass pie plate. Cover with plastic wrap; refrigerate until ready to serve.

2. Preheat oven to 375°F. Cut each breadstick in half crosswise; place on ungreased baking sheet. Make 3 slits in one end of each breadstick half to resemble fingers. Cut small piece of dough from other end; press dough piece onto "hand" to resemble thumb. Bake 8 to 10 minutes or until golden brown.

3. Just before serving, sprinkle dip with cracker crumbs; serve with breadstick "hands," vegetables or fruit. Garnish as desired.

Makes 12 to 16 servings

Jack-o'-Lantern Snacks

1 package (8 ounces) cream cheese, softened
  Red and yellow food coloring
8 large slices dark pumpernickel bread
1 small green bell pepper
  Sliced Genoa salami

1. Place cream cheese in small bowl. Add 8 drops red and 6 drops yellow food coloring to turn cream cheese orange. Mix well and adjust color as desired.

2. Toast bread and allow to cool. Using large pumpkin cookie cutter or metal 1-cup measure, cut a round shape from each slice of toast leaving "stem" on top. Spread cream cheese over toast to edges. Cut "stems" from green pepper and place over stem on toast. Cut triangle "eyes" and mouth with several "teeth" from sliced salami. Arrange over each pumpkin toast.

Makes 8 servings

Witches' Snack Hats

1 package (18 ounces)
  refrigerated sugar
  cookie dough
¼ cup unsweetened cocoa
  powder
1½ cups semisweet chocolate
  chips, divided
16 ice cream sugar cones
⅓ cup butter
3 cups dry cereal (mixture
  of puffed corn, bite-
  size wheat and toasted
  oat cereal)
½ cup roasted pumpkin
  seeds
½ cup chopped dried
  cherries or raisins
1⅓ cups powdered sugar
  Assorted colored sugars
  and decors

1. Preheat oven to 350°F. Grease cookie sheets; set aside. Remove dough from wrapper. Combine dough and cocoa powder in large bowl; mix until well blended. Evenly divide dough into 16 pieces; shape into balls. Flatten each ball onto prepared cookie sheet into 3½- to 4-inch circle. Bake 6 to 8 minutes or until set. Cool on cookie sheets 5 minutes. Remove to wire racks; cool completely.

2. Line large tray with waxed paper. Place 1 cup chocolate chips in small microwavable bowl. Microwave on HIGH at 30-second intervals until melted, stirring after each interval. Coat outside of sugar cones with chocolate using clean pastry brush. Stand up on prepared tray; let set.

3. Place remaining ½ cup chocolate chips and butter in small microwavable bowl. Microwave on HIGH at 30-second intervals until melted, stirring after each interval. Stir mixture to blend well. Place cereal, pumpkin seeds and cherries in large bowl. Pour chocolate mixture over cereal mixture and stir until thoroughly coated. Sprinkle mixture with powdered sugar, ⅓ cup at a time, carefully folding and mixing until thoroughly coated.

4. Fill cone with snack mix. Brush cone edge with melted chocolate; attach to center of cookie and let set. Repeat with remaining cones, snack mix and cookies. Decorate hats as desired with melted chocolate, colored sugars and decors.

Makes 16 servings

Hint: To use these hats as place cards, simply write each guest's name on the hat with melted white chocolate, frosting or decorating gel.

Coffin Cake

1 loaf (16 ounces) pound
    cake, thawed if frozen
4 graham crackers
1 container (1 pound)
    caramel frosting
½ pound assorted
    Halloween candies
5 to 10 gummy worms

1. Cut cake loaf to resemble coffin by cutting 1-inch triangle from 1 corner of cake. Cut opposite corner to match; this will be the top end of coffin. Cut long, narrow triangles (1×4-inches) off bottom corners to form bottom end.

2. Slice ½-inch layer off top of cake horizontally to form lid; set aside. Leaving ½-inch border, cut around inside edge of cake and scoop out some of interior. Cut graham crackers to fit onto cake sides; use frosting to attach graham cracker "boards" to outer sides of cake. Frost top of cake, if desired.

3. Fill inside of cake with candy and gummy worms, allowing some to spill out over edges. Set lid on cake at slight angle.

Makes 8 servings

•super suggestion

Cake looks great atop chocolate cookie crumbs, on a wooden cutting board, with a small spoon as a shovel in a pile of "dirt" crumbs next to coffin.

Doodle Bug Cupcakes

1 package (18¼ ounces)
    white cake mix *without*
    pudding in the mix
1 cup sour cream
3 eggs
⅓ cup water
⅓ cup vegetable oil
1 teaspoon vanilla
1½ cups prepared cream
    cheese frosting
    Red, yellow, blue and
    green food coloring
    Red licorice strings, cut
    into 2-inch pieces
    Assorted round
    decorating candies

1. Preheat oven to 350°F. Line 24 standard (2½-inch) muffin cups with paper baking cups.

2. Beat cake mix, sour cream, eggs, water, oil and vanilla in large bowl with electric mixer at low speed about 1 minute or until blended. Increase speed to medium; beat 1 to 2 minutes or until smooth.

3. Fill muffin cups about two-thirds full. Bake about 20 minutes or until toothpick inserted into centers comes out clean. Cool cupcakes in pans on wire racks 5 minutes. Remove to wire racks; cool completely.

4. Divide frosting evenly between 4 small bowls. Add one food coloring to each bowl, one drop at a time, to reach desired shades; stir each frosting until well blended. Frost tops of cupcakes with desired shades.

5. Use toothpick to make three small holes on opposite sides of each cupcake, making six holes total. Insert licorice piece into each hole for "legs." Decorate tops of cupcakes with assorted candies.

Makes 24 cupcakes

DOODLE BUG CUPCAKES

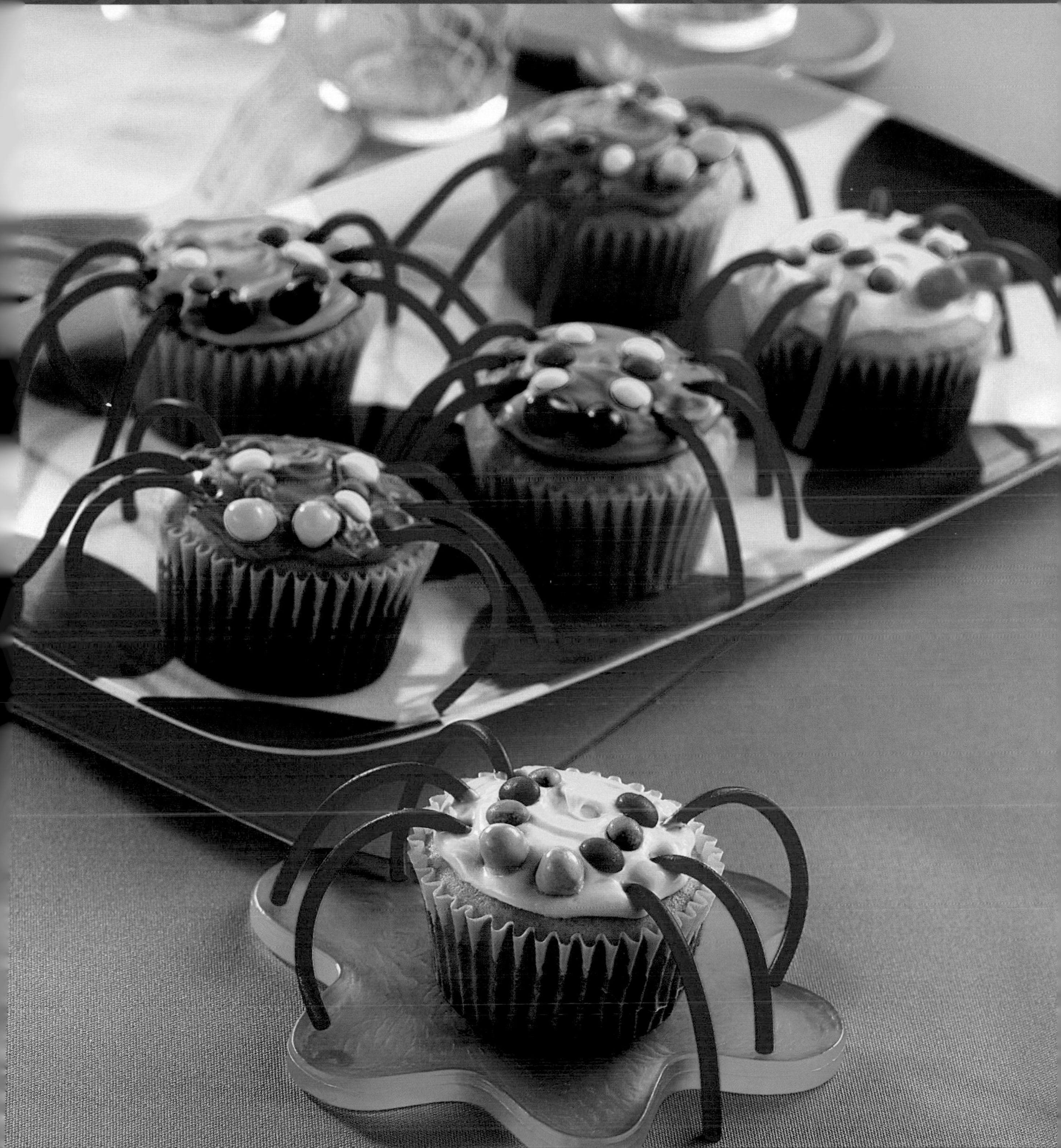

PB & J Sandwich Cake

1 package (18¼ ounces) white cake mix, plus ingredients to prepare mix
¾ cup powdered sugar
5 tablespoons peanut butter
2 to 3 tablespoons whipping cream or milk
1 tablespoon butter, softened
½ cup strawberry or grape jam

1. Preheat oven to 350°F. Grease two 8-inch square baking pans. Prepare cake mix according to package directions. Spread batter in prepared pans.

2. Bake 30 minutes or until toothpick inserted into centers comes out clean. Cool in pans on wire racks 30 minutes. Remove to wire racks; cool completely.

3. Carefully slice off browned tops of both cakes to create flat, even layers. Place one layer on serving plate, cut side up.

4. Beat powdered sugar, peanut butter, 2 tablespoons cream and butter in medium bowl with electric mixer at medium speed until light and creamy. Add remaining 1 tablespoon cream, if necessary, to reach spreading consistency. Gently spread peanut butter filling over cut side of cake layer on serving plate. Spread jam over filling. Top with second cake layer, cut side up.

5. Cut cake in half diagonally to resemble sandwich. To serve, cut into thin slices across the diagonal using serrated knife.

Makes 12 servings

Give Me S'more Muffins

Prep Time: 25 minute

2 cups graham cracker
  crumbs
⅓ cup sugar
⅓ cup mini chocolate chips
2 teaspoons baking powder
1 egg
¾ cup milk
24 milk chocolate candy
  kisses, unwrapped
2 cups mini marshmallows

1. Preheat oven to 350°F. Line mini (1¾-inch) muffin cups with paper baking cups. Set aside.

2. Combine graham cracker crumbs, sugar, chocolate chips and baking powder in medium bowl. Whisk egg into milk and stir into crumb mixture until well blended.

3. Spoon batter into prepared pan, filling each cup about half full. Press chocolate kiss into each cup. Press 4 marshmallows into tops of each muffin. Bake 10 to 12 minutes or until marshmallows are lightly browned. Cool 10 minutes in pan. Remove to wire racks; cool completely. *Makes about 2 dozen mini muffins*

"M&M's"® Family Party Mix

2 tablespoons butter or
  margarine*
¼ cup honey*
2 cups favorite grain cereal
  or 3 cups granola
1 cup coarsely chopped
  nuts
1 cup thin pretzel pieces
1 cup raisins
2 cups "M&M's"®
  Chocolate Mini
  Baking Bits

For a drier mix, eliminate butter and honey. Simply combine dry ingredients and do not bake.

Preheat oven to 300°F. In large saucepan over low heat, melt butter; add honey until well blended. Remove from heat and add cereal, nuts, pretzel pieces and raisins, stirring until all pieces are evenly coated. Spread mixture onto ungreased cookie sheet and bake about 10 minutes. Do not overbake. Spread mixture onto waxed paper and allow to cool completely. In large bowl combine mixture and "M&M's"® Chocolate Mini Baking Bits. Store in tightly covered container. *Makes about 6 cups snack mix*

Hershey's Easy Chocolate Cracker Snacks

1²/₃ cups (10-ounce package)
   HERSHEY'S Mint
   Chocolate Chips*
2 cups (12-ounce package)
   HERSHEY'S Semi-Sweet
   Chocolate Chips
2 tablespoons shortening
   (do not use butter,
   margarine, spread
   or oil)
60 to 70 round buttery
   crackers (about ½
   1-pound box)

*2 cups (11.5-ounce package)
HERSHEY'S Milk Chocolate
Chips and ¼ teaspoon pure
peppermint extract can be
substituted for mint chocolate
chips.*

1. Line several trays or cookie sheets with wax paper.

2. Place mint chocolate chips, chocolate chips and shortening in large microwave-safe bowl. Microwave at HIGH (100%) 1 minute; stir. Continue heating 30 seconds at a time, stirring after each heating, until chips are melted and mixture is smooth when stirred.

3. Drop crackers into chocolate mixture one at a time. Using tongs, push cracker into chocolate so that it is covered completely. (If chocolate begins to thicken, reheat 10 to 20 seconds in microwave.) Remove from chocolate, tapping lightly on edge of bowl to remove excess chocolate. Place on prepared tray. Refrigerate until chocolate hardens, about 20 minutes. For best results, store tightly covered in refrigerator.

Makes about 5½ dozen crackers

Peanut Butter and Milk Chocolate: Use 1²/₃ cups (10-ounce package) REESE'S® Peanut Butter Chips, 2 cups (11.5-ounce package) HERSHEY'S Milk Chocolate Chips and 2 tablespoons shortening. Proceed as directed.

White Chip and Toffee: Melt 2 bags (12 ounces each) HERSHEY'S Premier White Chips and 2 tablespoons shortening. Dip crackers; before coating hardens sprinkle with HEATH® BITS 'O BRICKLE® Toffee Bits.

Kid Kabobs with Cheesy Mustard Dip

Prep Time: 15 minutes

Dip
- 1 container (8 ounces) whipped cream cheese
- ¼ cup milk
- 3 tablespoons *French's®* Spicy Brown Mustard or Honey Mustard
- 2 tablespoons mayonnaise
- 2 tablespoons minced green onions

Kabobs
- ½ pound deli luncheon meat or cooked chicken and turkey, cut into 1-inch cubes
- ½ pound Swiss, Cheddar or Monterey Jack cheese, cut into 1-inch cubes
- 2 cups cut-up assorted vegetables such as broccoli, carrots, peppers, cucumbers and celery
- 16 wooden picks, about 6-inches long

1. Combine ingredients for dip in medium bowl; mix until well blended.

2. To make kabobs, place cubes of meat, cheese and chunks of vegetables on wooden picks.

3. Serve kabobs with dip. *Makes 8 servings (about 1¼ cups dip)*

·super suggestion · · · · · · · · · · ·

Have your children help make these silly kabobs. Make sure they eat them carefully, since the toothpicks have sharp points.

Cinnamon Toast Poppers

2 tablespoons butter
6 cups fresh bread* cubes
(1-inch cubes)
1 tablespoon plus
1½ teaspoons sugar
½ teaspoon ground
cinnamon

Use a firm sourdough, whole wheat or semolina bread.

1. Preheat oven to 325°F. Melt butter in Dutch oven or large skillet over low heat. Add bread cubes and toss to coat; remove from heat. Combine sugar and cinnamon in small bowl. Sprinkle over bread cubes; stir well.

2. Spread bread cubes in one layer on ungreased baking sheet. Bake 25 minutes or until bread is golden and fragrant, stirring once or twice. Serve warm or at room temperature.

Makes 12 servings

Twisted Dunkers

Prep Time: 15 minutes • **Bake Time:** 15 minutes

¾ cup finely grated
Parmesan cheese
½ teaspoon dried oregano
¼ teaspoon garlic powder
1 egg, beaten
1 tablespoon water
1 package (11 ounces)
refrigerated breadstick
dough
¾ cup pizza sauce

1. Preheat oven to 375°F. Grease large baking sheet. Set aside.

2. Combine Parmesan, oregano and garlic powder in shallow dish. Combine egg and water in another shallow dish.

3. Unroll breadstick dough. Separate into 12 pieces. Dip each breadstick in egg mixture. Roll in Parmesan mixture. Twist each breadstick twice. Place on prepared baking sheet. Bake 12 minutes or until golden brown.

4. Meanwhile, heat pizza sauce in small microwavable bowl on HIGH 15 seconds or until warm. Serve warm breadsticks with warm pizza sauce.

Makes 6 servings (2 breadsticks each)

Cheesy Ham Biscuits

Nonstick cooking spray
1 can (12 ounces)
    buttermilk biscuits
2 tablespoons mayonnaise
1½ tablespoons honey
    mustard
12 ham cubes, diced ¾ inch
    thick
36 Cheddar cheese cubes

1. Preheat oven to 400°F.

2. Spray 10 standard (2½-inch) muffin cups with cooking spray. Place one biscuit in each of 10 sections.

3. Combine mayonnaise and mustard in small bowl. Stir until well blended.

4. Using thumbs, press down to make deep indentation in each biscuit. Spoon equal amounts of mayonnaise mixture in each, about 1 teaspoon per biscuit. Top each with 1 ham cube and 3 cheese cubes.

5. Place muffin pan on foil-lined oven rack. Bake 12 minutes or until biscuits are golden, puffed slightly and overflowing with cheese.

6. Remove from oven and let stand 3 minutes before removing from pan. Cool slightly; serve warm.

Makes 10 biscuits

CHEESY HAM BISCUITS

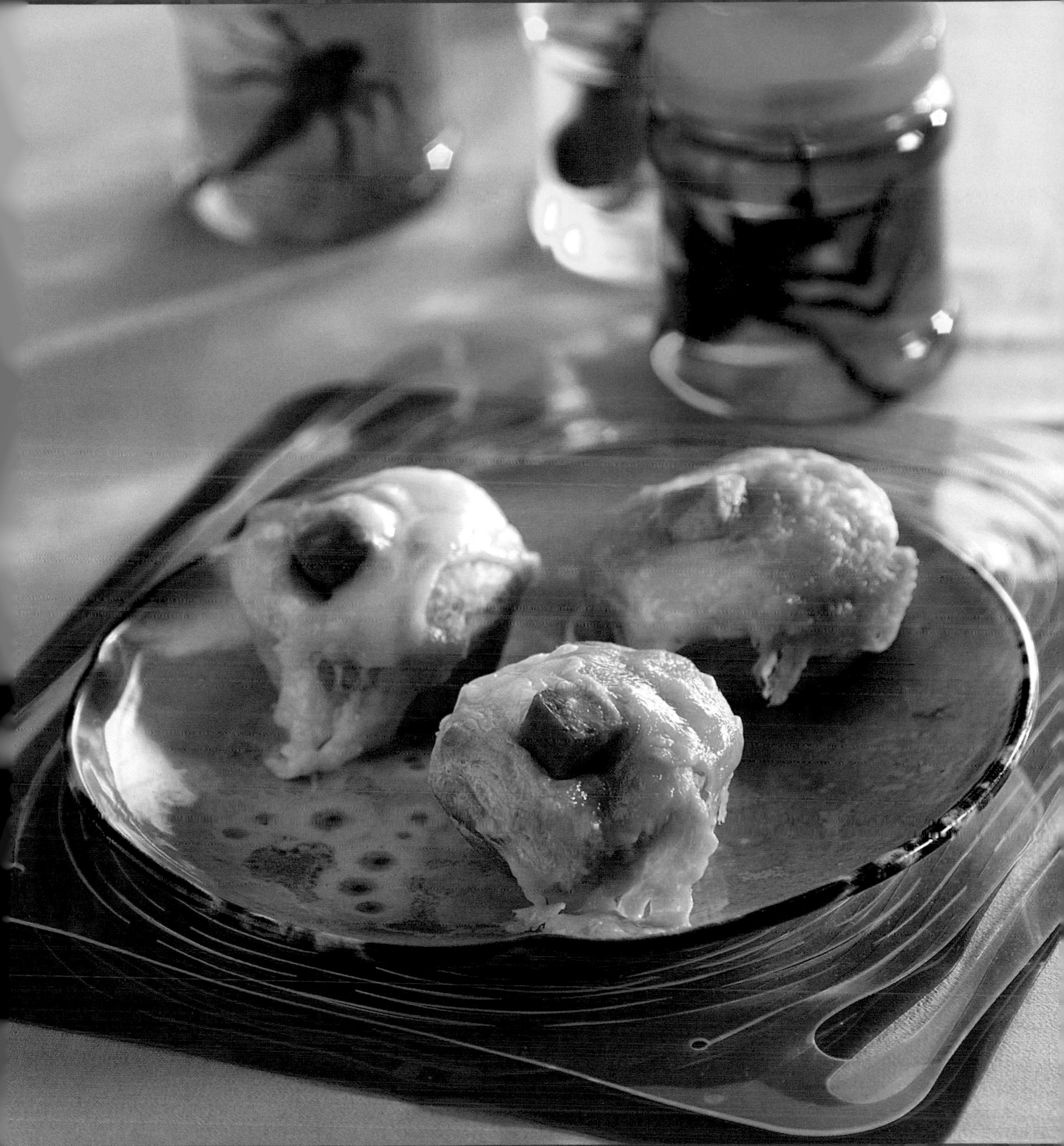

Super-Lucky Cereal Treats

40 marshmallows
¼ cup (½ stick) butter
6 cups oat cereal with marshmallow bits
Irish-themed candy cake decorations

1. Line 8-inch square pan with aluminum foil, leaving 2-inch overhang on 2 sides. Generously grease or spray with nonstick cooking spray.

2. Melt marshmallows and butter in medium saucepan over medium heat 3 minutes or until melted and smooth, stirring constantly. Remove from heat.

3. Add cereal; stir until completely coated. Spread in prepared pan; press evenly onto bottom using rubber spatula. Let cool 10 minutes. Using foil overhangs as handles, remove treats from pan. Cut into 16 bars. Press candy decorations onto top of treats.

Makes 16 treats

Critter Munch

1½ cups animal cracker cookies
½ (6-ounce) package Cheddar or original flavor goldfish-shaped crackers (1½ cups)
1 cup dried tart cherries
1 cup candy-coated chocolate candies
1 cup honey-roasted peanuts

Put cookies, goldfish crackers, cherries, candies and peanuts in a large mixing bowl.

Carefully stir with a spoon.

Store in a tightly covered container at room temperature.

Makes 6 cups

Favorite recipe from ***Cherry Marketing Institute***

SUPER-LUCKY CEREAL TREATS

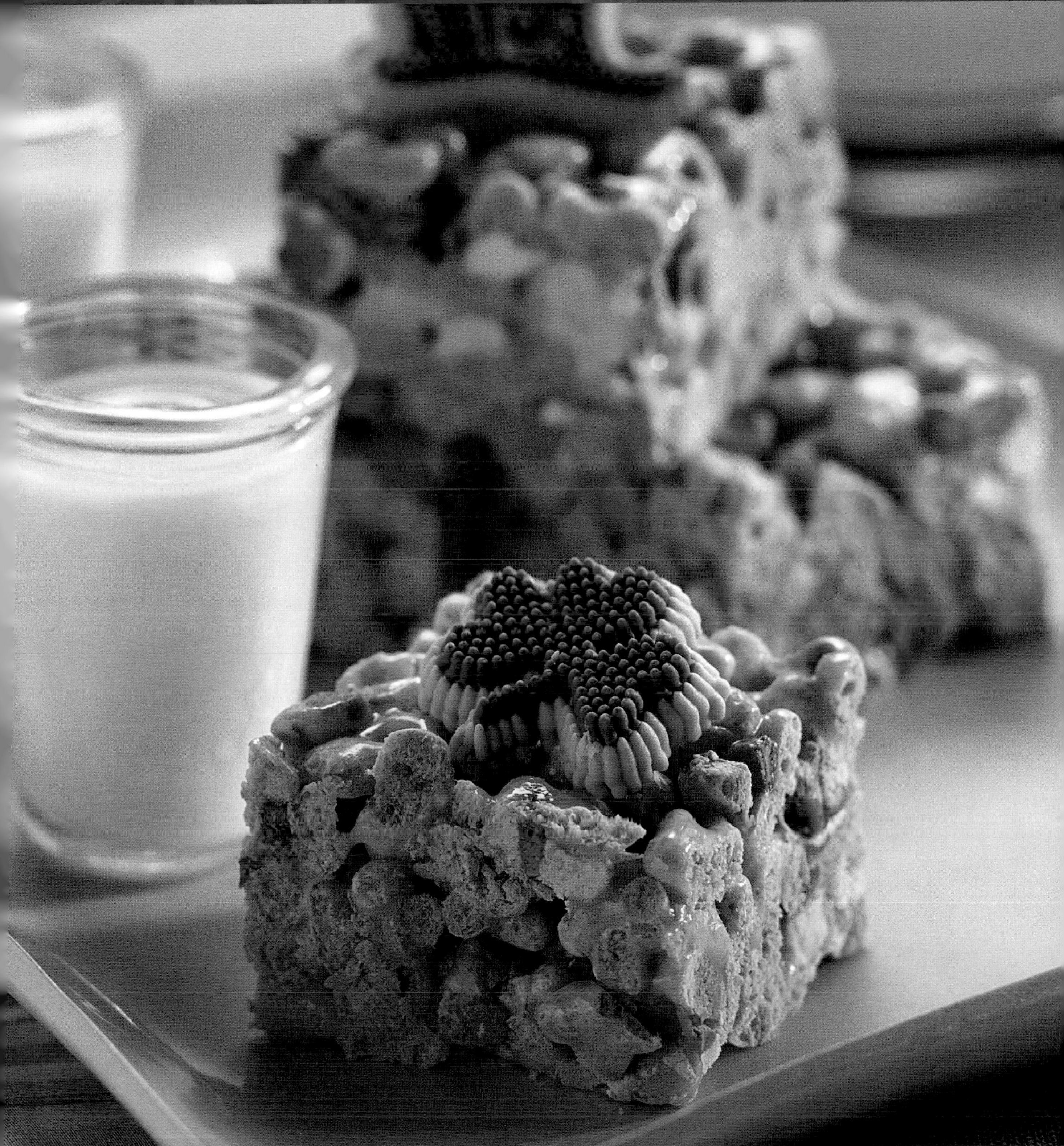

Pizza Cake

1 package (18¼ ounces)
    yellow cake mix, plus
    ingredients to prepare
    mix
1 container (16 ounces)
    white frosting
    Red food coloring
    Orange round gummy
    candies
    Green sugar-coated sour
    gummy strips, cut into
    small pieces
    Purple round sour gummy
    rings
    White candy-coated
    licorice strips

1. Preheat oven to 350°F. Grease and flour 12-inch deep-dish pizza pan. Prepare cake mix according to package directions. Pour batter into prepared pan.

2. Bake 18 to 25 minutes or until toothpick inserted into center comes out clean. Cool cake in pan about 15 minutes. Remove to wire racks; cool completely.

3. Combine frosting and food coloring in medium bowl until desired shade of red is reached. Place cake on serving plate; frost top of cake to within ¼ inch of edge.

4. Arrange candies over cake to resemble "pizza toppings" and "cheese."

Makes 12 servings

Chunky Chews

Prep Time: 20 minutes

1 cup powdered sugar,
    divided
½ cup chunky peanut butter
2 tablespoons honey
2 tablespoons coconut, plus
    additional for coating
2 tablespoons raisins
2 tablespoons chopped nuts

1. Combine ½ cup powdered sugar, peanut butter and honey in medium bowl. Mix until well blended. (Mixture may be crumbly.) Add coconut and raisins; mix well. Form dough into ¾ inch balls.

2. Coat balls in remaining ½ cup powdered sugar, additional coconut or chopped nuts. Place chews in paper candy wrappers, if desired. To store; place in airtight container up to 4 days.

Makes about 3 dozen chews

Cooking for Kids

Table of Contents

Cooking for Kids

Breakfast Cones

Prep Time: 10 minutes • **Baking Time:** 15 minutes

18 flat bottom ice cream
    cones
1 package (about
    15 ounces) cinnamon
    streusel muffin mix
¾ cup milk
2 eggs
¼ cup vegetable oil
½ cup crisp rice cereal
    (optional)
⅓ cup strawberry jam

1. Preheat oven to 400°F. Stand ice cream cones up in standard (2½-inch) muffin cups; set aside. Open muffin mix package; set aside streusel topping packet.

2. Combine muffin mix, milk, eggs and oil in medium bowl just until mixed. Stir in cereal, if desired. Spoon about 2 tablespoons batter into each ice cream cone. Sprinkle 1 teaspoon streusel topping over batter in each cone. Bake 15 minutes or until lightly browned and toothpick inserted into centers comes out clean.

3. Top each cone with ½ teaspoon jam. Serve warm or at room temperature. Store leftovers in airtight container.

Makes 18 cones

Hawaiian Breakfast Pizza

Prep Time: 5 minutes

2 teaspoons barbecue sauce
   or pineapple jam
1 English muffin, split in
   half and toasted
1 slice (1 ounce) smoked
   ham, diced
½ cup pineapple chunks
2 tablespoons shredded
   Cheddar cheese

1. Spread barbecue sauce over each muffin half; place on foil-lined toaster oven tray. Sprinkle ham and pineapple chunks over muffin halves; top with cheese.

2. Toast about 2 minutes or until cheese is melted.

Makes 1 serving

Note: To heat in a conventional oven, preheat oven to 400°F; heat muffin halves on a foil-lined baking sheet about 5 minutes or until cheese is melted.

Stuffed Picante Muffins

4 eggs
2 tablespoons fat-free
   (skim) milk
½ cup chopped leftover
   ham or 3 slices
   Canadian bacon
   (3 ounces), chopped
   Nonstick cooking spray
4 English muffin halves,
   lightly toasted
½ cup (2 ounces) shredded
   Cheddar cheese
¼ cup picante sauce

1. In medium bowl, combine eggs and milk; whisk or have your child beat with an egg beater, until well blended.

2. Place nonstick skillet over medium heat until hot. Coat skillet with cooking spray, add egg mixture, sprinkle evenly with ham pieces and cook 2 minutes. When eggs are set around the edges, cook and stir until eggs are fluffy and firm.

3. Remove from heat; spoon equal amounts (about ½ cup each) of egg mixture on top of each muffin half. Sprinkle each with 2 tablespoons cheese and top with 1 tablespoon picante sauce.

Makes 4 servings

Breakfast Banana Split

Prep Time: 5 minutes

1 banana
3 strawberries, sliced
¼ cup fresh blueberries
1 container (6 ounces)
    "fruit on the bottom"
    reduced-fat strawberry
    yogurt, mixed
1 tablespoon granola
1 maraschino cherry

Peel banana; slice in half lengthwise. Place banana in serving dish and separate halves. Place half strawberries and blueberries on banana slices. Gently spoon yogurt over berries. Top with remaining berries; sprinkle with granola. Garnish with cherry.

Makes 1 serving

Apple Orchard Pancakes

¾ cup packed brown sugar
¼ cup vegetable oil
1½ cups milk
2 eggs
2½ cups all-purpose flour
2 teaspoons baking powder
1¼ teaspoon ground
    cinnamon
½ teaspoon baking soda
¼ teaspoon salt
¾ cup chopped dried apples
½ cup golden raisins
1 teaspoon butter
    Maple syrup (optional)

1. Beat brown sugar and oil in large bowl with electric mixer at medium speed. Beat in milk and eggs.

2. Combine flour, baking powder, cinnamon, baking soda and salt in medium bowl. Beat flour mixture into egg mixture just until blended. Stir in dried apples and raisins.

3. Lightly coat griddle with butter. Heat over medium heat until hot. Pour about ¼ cup batter onto griddle for each pancake. Cook until bubbles form and bottom of pancakes are brown; turn and cook about 2 minutes or until brown and cooked through. Repeat with remaining batter. Serve pancakes with syrup, if desired.

Makes about 20 pancakes

BREAKFAST BANANA SPLIT

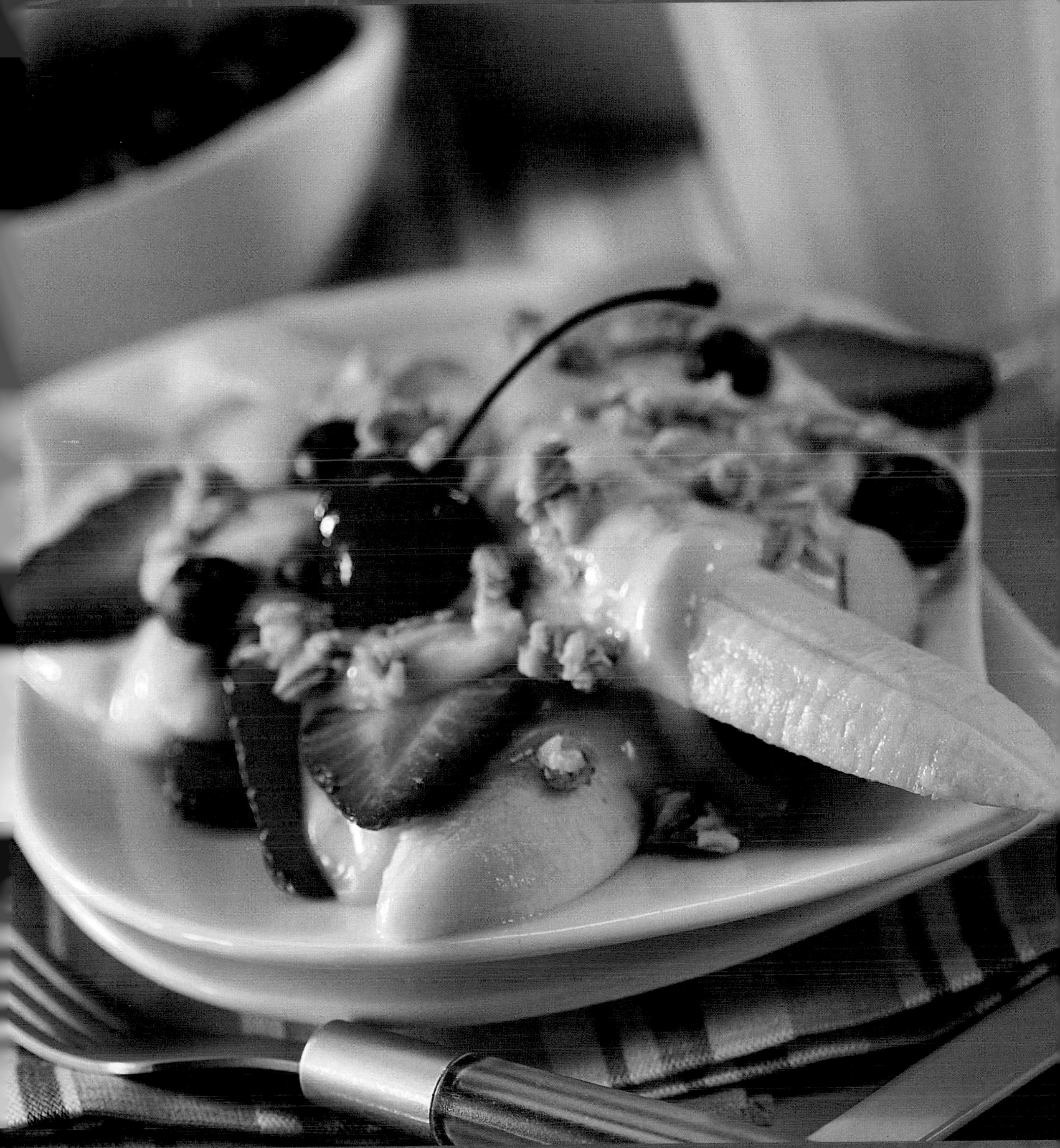

Apricot Mini Muffins

¼ cup (½ stick) butter,
    melted and cooled
¼ cup sugar
1 egg
1 tablespoon milk
½ teaspoon vanilla
¾ cup all-purpose flour
¼ cup finely chopped dried
    apricots
⅛ teaspoon baking powder
⅛ teaspoon baking soda
    Pinch ground nutmeg
    Pinch salt

1. Preheat oven to 350°F. Spray 12 mini (1¾-inch) muffin cups with nonstick cooking spray; set aside.

2. Beat butter and sugar in medium bowl with electric mixer at medium speed. Beat in egg, milk, and vanilla. Combine remaining ingredients in small bowl. Beat flour mixture into butter mixture just until blended. Spoon about 1 tablespoon batter into each prepared muffin cup.

3. Bake 12 to 15 minutes or until toothpick inserted into centers comes out clean.

Makes 12 mini muffins

super suggestion

Remove muffins from their cups immediately after baking and cool them on a wire rack. They are best when served warm. Stored in an airtight plastic bag, muffins will stay fresh for several days. For longer storage, wrap and freeze. To reheat, wrap frozen muffins in foil and heat in a 350°F oven for 15 to 20 minutes. For best flavor, use frozen muffins within one month.

Stuffed French Toast Sandwiches

Prep Time: 15 minutes

8 slices whole wheat or
white bread
4 thin slices ham (1 ounce
each)
3 eggs
¾ cup reduced-fat (2%)
milk
1 tablespoon sugar
Nonstick cooking spray
4 tablespoons butter
(optional)
Pancake syrup, warmed

1. Place 4 slices of bread on baking pan. Cover each bread slice with 1 slice of ham; top with remaining bread slices.

2. Whisk eggs, milk and sugar in medium bowl. Pour egg mixture over sandwiches. Allow sandwiches to stand at room temperature, about 5 minutes, turning once, to absorb egg mixture.

3. Spray large skillet with cooking spray; heat over medium heat. Cook sandwiches, in batches, if necessary, about 2 minutes on each side or until golden brown. Serve each sandwich with 1 tablespoon butter, if desired, and syrup. *Makes 4 servings*

Breakfast Tacos

Prep Time: 10 minutes

2 eggs
  Nonstick cooking spray
6 mini taco shells or
  2 regular-sized taco
  shells
½ teaspoon taco seasoning
  mix
2 tablespoons shredded
  Cheddar cheese or
  cheese sauce
2 tablespoons mild salsa
2 tablespoons chopped
  fresh parsley
  Sliced green onion and
  shredded lettuce
  (optional)

1. Beat eggs in small bowl until well blended. Heat small skillet coated with cooking spray over medium-low heat. Pour eggs into skillet; cook, stirring often, until desired doneness. Sprinkle taco seasoning over eggs.

2. Heat taco shells according to package directions; cool slightly. Spoon egg mixture into taco shells. Top each taco with 1 teaspoon *each* cheese, salsa and parsley. Add green onion and lettuce, if desired.

Makes 2 servings

super suggestion

Refrigerate eggs immediately after purchasing. To prevent them from absorbing odors from other foods, store them in the original carton. For best flavor, use eggs within a week after purchasing. However, they will keep for five weeks after the packing date without loss of nutrients or functional properties.

Apple and Cheese Pockets

2 medium to large Golden
  Delicious apples,
  peeled, cored and
  finely chopped (2 cups)
2 cups (8 ounces) shredded
  sharp Cheddar cheese
2 tablespoons apple jelly
¼ teaspoon curry powder
1 package (about
  16 ounces) refrigerated
  reduced-fat large
  biscuits (8 biscuits)

1. Preheat oven to 350°F. Line baking sheet with parchment paper; set aside.

2. Combine apples, cheese, apple jelly and curry powder in large bowl and stir well.

3. Roll out one biscuit on lightly floured surface to 6½-inch circle. Place ½ cup apple mixture in center. Fold biscuit over filling to form semicircle; press to seal tightly. Place on baking sheet. Repeat with remaining biscuits and filling. Bake 15 to 18 minutes or until biscuits are golden and filling is hot.

4. To keep hot for lunch, place in vacuum container and close. Or, reheat pockets in microwave about 30 seconds on **HIGH** until hot.

Makes 8 servings

Note: Refrigerate leftovers up to two days or freeze up to one month.

Tip: Preheat vacuum container with boiling water; drain and dry before use.

Super Peanut Butter Sandwiches

Prep Time: 15 minutes

⅔ cup peanut butter
2 tablespoons toasted
    wheat germ
1 tablespoon honey
8 slices firm-texture whole
    wheat or multi-grain
    bread
1 ripe banana, sliced
½ cup cholesterol-free egg
    substitute or two eggs,
    beaten
⅓ cup orange juice
1 tablespoon grated orange
    peel
1 tablespoon butter or
    margarine

1. Combine peanut butter, wheat germ and honey in small bowl. Spread evenly on one side of each bread slice.

2. Place banana slices on top of peanut butter mixture on four slices of bread. Top with remaining bread slices, peanut butter side down. Lightly press together.

3. Combine egg substitute, orange juice and orange peel in shallow dish. Dip sandwiches in egg mixture, coating both sides.

4. Melt butter in large nonstick skillet. Cook sandwiches over medium heat until golden brown, turning once. Serve immediately.

Makes 4 servings

Finger-Licking Chicken Salad

½ cup diced roasted skinless
    chicken
¼ cup drained mandarin
    orange segments
¼ cup red seedless grapes
½ stalk celery, cut into
    1-inch pieces
2 tablespoons lemon
    fat-free sugar-free
    yogurt
1 tablespoon reduced-fat
    mayonnaise
¼ teaspoon reduced-sodium
    soy sauce
⅛ teaspoon pumpkin pie
    spice or cinnamon

1. Toss together chicken, oranges, grapes and celery in plastic container; cover.

2. For dipping sauce, combine yogurt, mayonnaise, soy sauce and pumpkin pie spice in small bowl. Place in small plastic container; cover.

3. Pack chicken mixture and dipping sauce in insulated bag with ice pack. To serve, dip chicken mixture into dipping sauce.

Makes 1 serving

Serving Suggestion: Thread the chicken on wooden skewers alternately with oranges, grapes and celery.

Diggity Dog Biscuits

3 cups dry biscuit mix
1 can (15 ounces)
    VEG•ALL® Original
    Mixed Vegetables,
    drained and mashed
2 hot dogs, chopped
½ cup shredded mild
    cheddar cheese
⅓ cup whole milk
1 tablespoon chopped fresh
    parsley
¼ teaspoon garlic salt

Preheat oven to 400°F.

Combine all ingredients into a large mixing bowl and stir until mixture forms a moist dough.

Drop about ⅓ cup of dough at a time onto a greased cookie sheet. Pat down lightly with the back of a spoon.

Bake for 10 to 15 minutes or until golden brown. Remove and let cool for 5 minutes. Serve.   *Makes 12 biscuits*

Cereal Trail Mix

2 cups multi-grain cereal
    squares
2 cups toasted oat ring
    cereal
1 cup cheese-flavored fish
    crackers
1 cup small pretzels
¾ cup raisins
½ cup peanuts or cashew
    pieces
½ cup dried banana slices

Combine all ingredients and serve.   *Makes 30 servings*

Favorite recipe from **Wheat Foods Council**

•super suggestion

Serving the tasty Diggity Dog Biscuits is a great way to get kids to eat vegetables without them knowing it. Serve with butter or ketchup.

Tic-Tac-Toe Sandwich

Prep Time: 5 minutes

2 teaspoons mayonnaise
1 slice whole wheat bread
1 slice white sandwich
   bread
1 slice cheese
1 slice deli ham
3 black or green olives

1. Spread 1 teaspoon mayonnaise on each slice of bread. Layer cheese and ham on one bread slice. Top with remaining slice. Trim crust from sandwich. Cut sandwich into 9 squares by cutting into thirds in each direction. Turn alternating pieces over to form checkerboard pattern.

2. Thinly slice 1 olive. Cut remaining 2 olives into strips. Place olive pieces on sandwich squares to form 'X's and 'O's.

Makes 1 sandwich

Mac and Cheese Bundles

2 cups cooked elbow
   macaroni
1 can (15 ounces)
   VEG•ALL® Original
   Mixed Vegetables,
   drained
4 ounces processed
   American cheese,
   cubed
½ cup diced ham
¼ cup half & half
1 tube (16 ounces) jumbo
   butter flavored biscuit
   dough (8 biscuits)
1 large egg, lightly beaten

Preheat oven to 375°F.

Combine all ingredients except biscuit dough and egg in a microwave-safe bowl. Microwave on high 2 minutes or until cheese is melted. Stir until pasta is well coated. Set aside to cool.

Roll out biscuits to ⅛-inch thick. Spoon about ⅓ cup of cooled macaroni mixture into the center of each biscuit. Bring corners together and pinch to seal.

Brush bundles with egg. Bake 15 to 20 minutes or until golden brown.

Makes 8 bundles

Ham, Apple and Cheese Turnovers

Prep Time: 15 minutes • **Bake Time:** 15 minutes

1¼ cups chopped cooked ham
¾ cup finely chopped red apple
¾ cup (3 ounces) shredded reduced-fat Cheddar cheese
1 tablespoon brown mustard (optional)
1 package (about 14 ounces) refrigerated pizza dough

1. Preheat oven to 400°F. Spray large baking sheet with nonstick cooking spray. Combine ham, apple, cheese and mustard in medium bowl; set aside.

2. Roll pizza dough into 15×10-inch rectangle on lightly floured surface. Cut into six (5-inch) squares. Top each square evenly with one sixth of ham mixture. Moisten edges with water. Fold dough over filling. Press edges to seal. Place on prepared baking sheet.

3. Prick tops of each turnover with fork. Bake about 15 minutes or until golden brown. Serve warm or allow to cool on wire rack 1 hour.

Makes 6 servings

Bear Bite Snack Mix

2 teaspoons sugar
¾ teaspoon ground cinnamon
¼ teaspoon ground nutmeg
1½ cups sweetened corn or oat cereal squares
1 cup teddy bear-shaped cookies
1 cup raisins
½ cup dried fruit bits or chopped mixed dried fruit
Nonstick cooking spray

1. Preheat oven to 350°F. Combine sugar, cinnamon and nutmeg in small bowl; mix well and set aside.

2. Combine cereal, cookies, raisins and dried fruit in medium bowl. Spread on jelly-roll pan. Generously spray with cooking spray. Sprinkle with half sugar mixture. Stir well. Spray again with cooking spray; sprinkle with remaining sugar mixture.

3. Bake 5 minutes; stir. Bake 5 minutes more; stir. Cool completely in pan on wire rack. Store in airtight container.

Makes 4 cups snack mix

HAM, APPLE AND CHEESE TURNOVERS

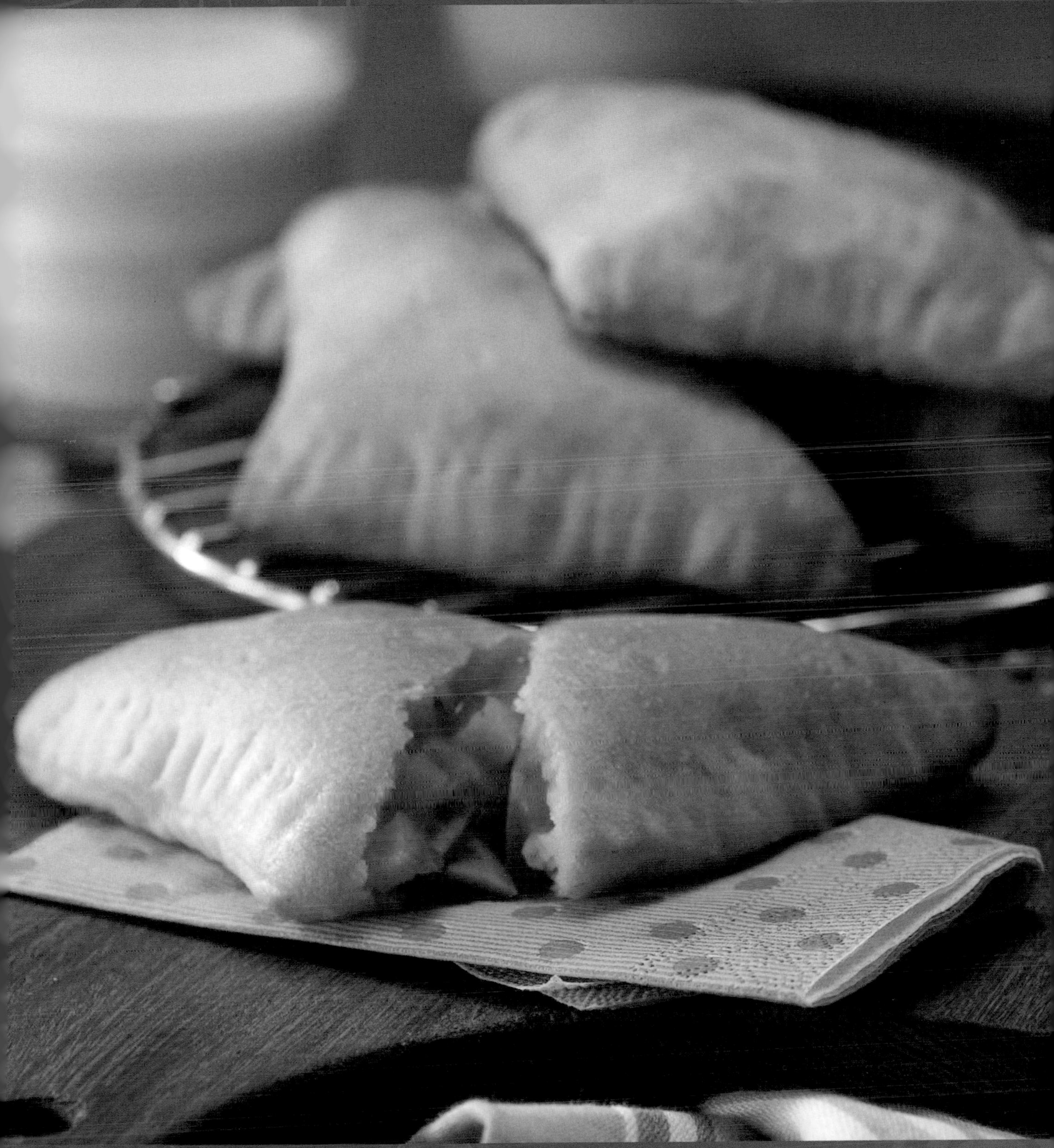

Peanut Butter-Apple Wraps

Prep Time: 5 minutes • **Chill Time:** 2 hours

¾ cup creamy peanut butter
4 (7-inch) whole wheat or
　spinach tortillas
¾ cup finely chopped apple
⅓ cup shredded carrot
⅓ cup low-fat granola
　without raisins
1 tablespoon toasted wheat
　germ

Spread peanut butter on one side of each tortilla. Sprinkle each tortilla evenly with apple, carrot, granola and wheat germ. Roll up tightly; cut in half. Serve immediately or refrigerate until ready to serve.

Makes 4 servings

Peanut Butter and Fruit Pita Pockets

1 large crisp apple, peeled,
　cored and finely diced
1 medium Bartlett pear,
　peeled, cored and
　finely diced
1½ teaspoons raisins
2 teaspoons orange juice
3 tablespoons chunky
　peanut butter
4 large lettuce leaves or
　8 large spinach leaves
2 whole wheat pitas, about
　2 ounces each

1. Combine diced apple, pear and raisins with orange juice and hold for 5 minutes. Add peanut butter and mix well.

2. Wash and dry lettuce or spinach leaves on paper towels. Tear lettuce into pita size pieces.

3. Warm pita in toaster on lowest color setting. Cut pita in half, and carefully open each half to make a pocket.

4. Line each pocket with lettuce or spinach leaves and spoon in equal portions of fruit and peanut butter mixture. Serve and enjoy.

Makes 4 snack portions or 2 meal portions

Note: A delicious and fun snack kids of all ages can make and enjoy...Sh-h-h-h, it's super healthy!

Favorite recipe from ***Chilean Fresh Fruit Association***

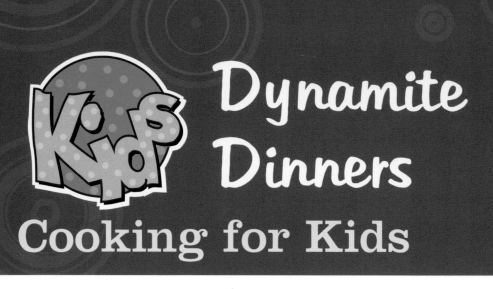

Earth's Core Meatballs

25 medium to large cherry tomatoes, halved and seeded

3 to 4 ounces part-skim mozzarella cheese, cut into ¼- to ½-inch cubes

2 eggs, divided

2 pounds ground beef

1½ cups Italian-style bread crumbs, divided

1 teaspoon salt

¾ teaspoon garlic powder

½ teaspoon black pepper

Cooked pasta and prepared pasta sauce (optional)

1. Preheat oven to 350°F. Line two baking sheets with foil and spray generously with nonstick cooking spray; set aside.

2. Insert 1 cheese cube into one tomato half; cover with another half to encase cheese.

3. Lightly beat one egg in large bowl. Add beef, ½ cup bread crumbs, salt, garlic powder and pepper; stir until well mixed. Shape 2 tablespoons beef mixture into rough 2-inch circle. Place cheese-filled tomato in center, then bring edges of circle together to completely encase tomato. Lightly roll meatball to form smooth ball. Place on prepared baking sheet. Repeat with remaining meat mixture, tomatoes and cheese.

4. Lightly beat remaining egg in medium shallow bowl. Place 1 cup bread crumbs in another shallow bowl. Dip meatballs, one at a time, into beaten egg; shake off excess and roll in bread crumbs. Return to baking sheet. Bake 35 minutes until meatballs are slightly crisp and are no longer pink, turning meatballs halfway through baking time. Serve on pasta with sauce, if desired.

Makes 12 servings

Mac and Cheese Toss

8 ounces oven baked deli
  ham, diced
4 cups prepared deli
  macaroni and cheese
  (1 quart)
½ cup frozen green peas,
  thawed
¼ cup milk or cream

1. Combine all ingredients in microwavable 2-quart casserole. Toss gently yet thoroughly to blend. Cover with plastic wrap.

2. Microwave on HIGH 3 minutes; stir. Microwave 1 minute more or until heated through.   *Makes 4 servings*

Note: To thaw peas quickly, place peas in a small colander and run under cold water 15 to 20 seconds or until thawed. Shake off liquid.

Octo-Dogs and Shells

4 hot dogs
1½ cups uncooked small shell
  pasta
1½ cups frozen mixed
  vegetables
1 cup prepared Alfredo
  sauce
  Prepared yellow mustard
  in squeeze bottle
  Cheese-flavored fish-
  shaped crackers

1. Lay 1 hot dog on cutting surface. Starting 1 inch from one end of hot dog, slice hot dog in half lengthwise. Roll hot dog ¼ turn. Starting 1 inch from same end, slice in half lengthwise again, making 4 segments connected at top. Slice each segment in half lengthwise, creating a total of 8 "legs." Repeat with remaining hot dogs.

2. Place hot dogs in medium saucepan; cover with water. Bring to a boil over medium-high heat. Remove from heat; set aside.

3. Prepare pasta according to package directions, stirring in vegetables during last 3 minutes of cooking. Drain; return to pan. Stir in Alfredo sauce. Heat over low heat until heated through. Divide pasta mixture between 4 plates.

4. Drain octo-dogs. Arrange one octo-dog on top of pasta mixture on each plate. Draw faces on "heads" of octo-dogs with mustard. Sprinkle crackers over pasta.   *Makes 4 servings*

Monster Mouths

1 teaspoon vegetable oil
1 medium onion, chopped
4 slices bacon, chopped
1 pound ground beef
2 medium plum tomatoes, seeded and chopped
4 slices American cheese, chopped
½ teaspoon salt
¼ teaspoon black pepper
½ (12-ounce) package jumbo pasta shells (about 18 shells), cooked and drained
Baby carrots, olives, red bell pepper, small pickles and cheese slices for decoration

1. Preheat oven to 350°F. Lightly grease 13×9-inch baking dish. Heat oil in large skillet over medium heat. Add onion and bacon; cook until onion is tender. Add beef; cook and stir about 5 minutes or until beef is no longer pink. Stir in tomatoes, cheese, salt and black pepper. Spoon mixture into cooked shells; place in prepared baking dish.

2. Cut carrots into very thin strips. Cut small slit in each olive; poke one end of thin carrot strip into each olive for "eye." Cut red bell pepper into "fangs." Slice pickle lengthwise to make "tongue." Cut cheese slice into zig-zag pattern for "teeth."

3. Bake 3 to 5 minutes or until hot; remove from oven. Decorate as desired with olive and carrot "eyes," bell pepper "fangs," pickle "tongue" and cheese "teeth." Serve immediately.

Makes about 6 servings

Chicken in a Nest

8 ounces angel hair pasta
1 can (10 ounces) chicken breast in water, drained
½ cup frozen peas
1 package (6 ounces) whipped cream cheese with garden vegetables or garlic and herb spread
2 tablespoons milk
1 teaspoon salt
⅛ teaspoon pepper

1. Cook pasta according to package directions; drain and keep warm.

2. Combine chicken, peas, cream cheese, milk, salt and pepper in medium saucepan. Stir mixture over low heat until heated through. (If sauce is too thick, add milk until desired consistency is reached.) To serve, swirl pasta in center of serving dish with large fork. Spoon chicken mixture into center of "nest."

Makes 4 servings

Shrimp Bowls

¾ cup short-grain rice
1 cup plus 2 tablespoons
   water
¼ teaspoon salt
1 tablespoon vegetable oil
2 cups frozen stir-fry
   vegetables
1 (12-ounce) package
   cooked baby shrimp,
   thawed if frozen and
   drained
⅓ to ½ cup prepared sweet
   and sour sauce
1 tablespoon soy sauce

1. Combine rice, water and salt in small saucepan with tight-fitting lid. Bring to a boil. Reduce heat to low; cover and cook 15 minutes or until rice is tender and liquid is absorbed. Keep warm.

2. Heat vegetable oil in large skillet over medium-high heat. Add vegetables; stir-fry 3 minutes or until crisp-tender. Stir in shrimp. Combine sweet and sour sauce, to taste, and soy sauce in small bowl. Pour over shrimp mixture; heat through.

3. To serve, mound rice onto 4 plates and press down in center to form "bowls." Spoon shrimp mixture into "bowls."

Makes 4 servings

String Cheese Spaghetti

Prep Time: 20 minutes

1 box (16 ounces)
   spaghetti, cooked and
   drained
1 jar (1 pound 10 ounces)
   RAGÚ® Organic Pasta
   Sauce, heated
2 cups diced mozzarella
   cheese (about
   8 ounces)

In large serving bowl, toss all ingredients. Garnish, if desired, with grated Parmesan cheese and chopped fresh parsley.

Makes 6 servings

Little Piggy Pies

Prep Time: 10 minutes • **Bake Time:** 11 minutes

2 cups frozen mixed
    vegetables (carrots,
    potatoes, peas, celery,
    green beans, corn,
    onions and/or lima
    beans)
1 can (10¾ ounces)
    reduced-fat condensed
    cream of chicken soup,
    undiluted
8 ounces chopped cooked
    chicken
⅓ cup water
⅓ cup plain low-fat yogurt
½ teaspoon dried thyme
¼ teaspoon poultry
    seasoning or ground
    sage
⅛ teaspoon garlic powder
1 package (10 biscuits)
    refrigerated buttermilk
    biscuits

1. Preheat oven to 400°F.

2. Remove 10 green peas from frozen mixed vegetables. Combine remaining vegetables, soup, chicken, water, yogurt, thyme, poultry seasoning and garlic powder in medium saucepan. Bring to a boil, stirring frequently. Cover; keep warm.

3. Press five biscuits into 3-inch circles. Cut each remaining biscuit into eight wedges. Place two wedges on top of each circle; fold points down to form "ears." Roll one wedge into small ball; place in center of each circle to form pig's "snout." Use tip of spoon handle to make indentations in snout for "nostrils." Place 2 reserved green peas on each circle for "eyes."

4. Spoon hot chicken mixture into 5 (10-ounce) custard cups. Place one biscuit "pig" on top of each. Place remaining biscuit wedges around each "pig" on top of chicken mixture, twisting one wedge "tail" for each. Bake 9 to 11 minutes or until biscuits are golden.

Makes 5 servings

Pork Chops with Chunky Chutney

Chunky Chutney

  4 small to medium apples,
     peeled, cored and
     coarsely chopped
     (4 cups)
  ¼ cup dried cranberries
  ¼ cup apple juice
  3 tablespoons sugar
  1 tablespoon minced
     crystallized ginger
     (optional)
  ¼ teaspoon ground
     cinnamon
  1 teaspoon lemon juice

Pork Chops

  2 strips bacon
  ¼ cup all-purpose flour
  ¼ teaspoon salt
  ¼ teaspoon black pepper
  ⅛ teaspoon paprika
  4 thin bone-in pork loin
     center-cut chops,
     trimmed of fat and
     meat around the bone
     to form a handle
  ½ cup chicken broth
  1 tablespoon lemon juice

1. To prepare Chunky Chutney, combine apples, cranberries, apple juice, sugar, ginger, if desired, and cinnamon in medium saucepan. Bring to a boil, stirring frequently. Reduce heat to low, cover and simmer 30 minutes or until apples are tender. Remove cover; increase heat to medium-high. Cook 1 to 2 minutes more or until some of liquid is cooked off. Stir in lemon juice.

2. Meanwhile, cook bacon in large skillet until crisp. Drain on paper towels. Reserve bacon drippings. Combine flour, salt, pepper and paprika in resealable food storage bag. Add pork chops; shake well to coat. Reserve remaining seasoned flour. Add pork chops to skillet; cook over medium heat 3 minutes per side. Remove from skillet. Pour off any drippings. Whisk together ½ teaspoon reserved seasoned flour, chicken broth and 1 tablespoon lemon juice. Stir into skillet; cook and stir, scraping up any browned bits until mixture is slightly thickened. Reduce heat to low. Return pork chops to skillet. Crumble bacon; add to skillet. Cover; simmer 5 minutes, turning once and basting with sauce. Serve with chutney.

Makes 4 servings

Crazy Creature Brownies

Prep Time: 5 minutes • **Bake Time:** 20 minutes • **Cool Time:** 1 hour

1¼ cups granulated sugar
¾ cup (1½ sticks) butter or margarine
½ cup unsweetened cocoa powder
½ cup cholesterol-free egg substitute
1 teaspoon vanilla
½ teaspoon baking soda
½ teaspoon baking powder
1½ cups all-purpose flour
1 cup low-fat buttermilk
3 cups powdered sugar, sifted
⅓ cup orange juice, apple juice or fat free milk
Food coloring (optional)

1. Preheat oven to 350°F. Line 15×10×1-inch jelly-roll pan with heavy-duty foil, extending foil over edges. Spray foil with nonstick cooking spray. Combine granulated sugar, butter and cocoa powder in large saucepan. Cook over low heat, stirring frequently, until butter is melted. Remove from heat.

2. Cool sugar mixture 5 minutes. Stir in egg substitute. Add vanilla, baking soda and baking powder; mix well. Alternately add flour and buttermilk, stirring until well blended after each addition. Spread into prepared pan. Bake 20 to 22 minutes or until toothpick inserted into center comes out clean.

3. Cool completely. Use foil to lift brownie out of pan. Remove foil; place brownie on cutting board. Cut into shapes with 2- to 3-inch animal shaped cookie cutters. Place on wire rack over waxed paper.

4. Combine powdered sugar and orange juice in small bowl. Tint with food coloring, if desired. Spread over brownies. Decorate as desired. Let stand about 20 minutes or until dry.

Makes 20 brownies

Jam Jam Bars

1 package (18¼ ounces) yellow or white cake mix with pudding in the mix
½ cup (1 stick) butter, melted
1 cup apricot preserves or raspberry jam
1 package (11 ounces) peanut butter and milk chocolate chips

1. Preheat oven to 350°F. Lightly spray 13×9-inch baking pan with nonstick cooking spray.

2. Pour cake mix into large bowl; stir in melted butter until well blended. (Dough will be lumpy.) Remove ½ cup dough and set aside. Press remaining dough evenly into prepared pan. Spread preserves in thin layer over dough in pan.

3. Place chips in medium bowl. Stir in reserved dough until well mixed. (Dough will remain in small lumps evenly distributed throughout chips.) Sprinkle mixture evenly over preserves.

4. Bake 20 minutes or until lightly browned and bubbling at edges. Cool completely in pan on wire rack.

Makes 24 bars

Ho Ho® Pudding

1 box (10 ounces) of HO HO'S®
2 packages (4-serving size each) instant chocolate pudding mix
4 cups milk
1 large tub (16 ounces) whipped topping

Cut Ho Ho's into circles, saving 1 Ho Ho. Mix pudding and milk according to package pudding directions and chill until thick. In large glass bowl, layer Ho Ho's, pudding and whipped topping, ending with whipped topping. Take remaining Ho Ho and slice in circles and place on top. Keep refrigerated until ready to eat.

Makes 10 to 12 servings

Tip: For Halloween, dye the whipped topping orange to create an orange and black dessert.

Cookie Crumb Sundae

1 package (about
    18 ounces) chocolate
    creme-filled sandwich
    cookies
4 cups milk, divided
1 package (4-serving size)
    cheesecake-flavored
    instant pudding mix
1 package (4-serving size)
    chocolate fudge-
    flavored instant
    pudding mix
1 container (8 ounces)
    frozen whipped
    topping, thawed
12 to 14 maraschino
    cherries, drained

1. Place cookies in large resealable food storage bag; crush with rolling pin. Place three fourths of crumbs in bottom of 13×9-inch baking pan.

2. Combine 2 cups milk and cheesecake-flavored pudding mix in large bowl. Prepare according to package directions. Pour pudding evenly over cookie crumbs.

3. Repeat with remaining 2 cups milk and chocolate fudge-flavored pudding mix. Pour evenly over cheesecake pudding.

4. Spread whipped topping over pudding. Sprinkle remaining one fourth of cookie crumbs over whipped topping. Top with maraschino cherries. Chill 1 hour before serving.

Makes 12 to 14 servings

•super suggestion

For birthday parties, holidays and picnics, make the dessert in individual disposable clean plastic cups. Decorate with festive colored sprinkles.

Wacky Watermelon

4 cups diced seedless
watermelon (1-inch
cubes)
¼ cup strawberry fruit
spread
2 cups fat-free vanilla
frozen yogurt
6 teaspoons mini chocolate
chips, divided

1. Place 2 cups watermelon and fruit spread in blender; cover, and pulse on low until smooth. Add remaining watermelon; cover, and again pulse until smooth. Add frozen yogurt, 1 cup at a time, pulsing until smooth after each addition.

2. Pour mixture into medium loaf pan (8×4 inches) and freeze 2 hours or until mixture begins to harden around edge of pan. Stir well until mixture is smooth and slushy. Evenly stir in 4½ teaspoons chocolate chips. Smooth out top of mixture with back of spoon. Sprinkle evenly with remaining 1½ teaspoons chocolate chips. Cover pan with foil and return to freezer. Freeze until solid, 6 hours or overnight.

3. To serve, place pan in warm water briefly; invert onto cutting board. Let stand 5 minutes on cutting board to soften slightly. Cut loaf into slices. Serve immediately.

4. Wrap leftover slices individually in plastic wrap and place upright in clean loaf pan. Store in freezer.

Makes 12 servings

Triple Chocolate Cups

2 cups low-fat chocolate
frozen yogurt
1 cup fat-free (skim) milk
2 tablespoons chocolate
syrup
¼ cup crushed chocolate
wafer crumbs
Whipped cream or
nondairy topping
Chocolate sprinkles or
decors (optional)

1. Line 24 mini (1¾-inch) muffin cups with paper baking cups. Combine chocolate syrup, frozen yogurt and milk in blender; cover. Blend on HIGH speed until smooth. Add chocolate wafer crumbs; cover and pulse on HIGH speed until mixed. Spoon mixture into prepared muffin cups, filling three-fourths full. Freeze 1 hour or until solid.

2. If liners sticks to muffin pan, thaw at room temperature 10 to 15 minutes or until liners can be easily removed. Just before serving, garnish with whipped cream and chocolate sprinkles. Freeze leftovers in airtight container. *Makes 24 cups*

Tip: Have your child help by filling the muffin liners or adding the sprinkles.

Cookie Sundae Cups

1 package (18 ounces)
refrigerated chocolate
chip cookie dough
6 cups ice cream, any
flavor
Ice cream topping, any
flavor
Whipped cream
Colored sprinkles

1. Preheat oven to 350°F. Lightly grease 18 standard (2½-inch) muffin cups.

2. Remove dough from wrapper. Shape dough into 18 balls; press onto bottoms and up sides of prepared muffin cups.

3. Bake 14 to 18 minutes or until golden brown. Cool in pans 10 minutes. Remove to wire rack; cool completely.

4. Place ⅓ cup ice cream in each cookie cup. Drizzle with ice cream topping. Top with whipped cream and colored sprinkles.
Makes 18 cups

Cookie Fondue

Cookie Dippers
1 package (18 ounces) refrigerated oatmeal raisin cookie dough
1 cup powdered sugar
1 egg

Chocolate Sauce
½ cup semisweet chocolate chips
¼ cup whipping cream

White Chocolate Sauce
½ cup white chocolate chips
¼ cup whipping cream

Strawberry-Marshmallow Sauce
¼ cup strawberry syrup
¼ cup marshmallow creme

1. For cookie dippers, preheat oven to 350°F. Grease cookie sheets.

2. Remove dough from wrapper; place in large bowl. Let dough stand at room temperature about 15 minutes.

3. Add powdered sugar and egg to dough; beat with electric mixer at medium speed until well blended. Drop dough by teaspoonfuls onto prepared cookie sheets.

4. Bake 8 minutes or until edges are lightly browned. Cool on cookie sheets 5 minutes. Remove to wire rack; cool completely.

5. For Chocolate Sauce, combine semisweet chocolate chips and cream in microwavable bowl. Microwave on HIGH 20 seconds; stir. Microwave on HIGH for additional 20-second intervals until chips are melted and mixture is smooth; stir well after each interval.

6. For White Chocolate Sauce, combine white chocolate chips and cream in microwavable bowl. Microwave on HIGH 20 seconds; stir. Microwave on HIGH for additional 20-second intervals until chips are melted and mixture is smooth; stir well after each interval.

7. For Strawberry-Marshmallow Sauce, mix strawberry syrup and marshmallow creme in small bowl; stir until smooth.

8. Serve cookie dippers with sauces.   *Makes 2½ dozen cookies*

Tip: Serve sauces in small bowls along with small bowls of chopped nuts, coconut and dried cranberries for "double" dipping.

Silly Snacks

Table of Contents

Silly Snacks

Happy Apple Salsa with Baked Cinnamon Pita Chips

2 teaspoons sugar
¼ teaspoon cinnamon
2 rounds pita bread, split
  Nonstick cooking spray
1 tablespoon jelly or jam
1 apple, diced
1 tablespoon finely diced
  celery
1 tablespoon finely diced
  carrot
1 tablespoon raisins
1 teaspoon lemon juice

1. Preheat oven to 350°F.

2. Combine sugar and cinnamon in small bowl. Set aside.

3. Cut pitas into wedges and place on a baking sheet. Spray lightly with cooking spray and sprinkle with cinnamon sugar mixture. Bake 10 minutes or until lightly browned; set aside to cool.

4. Meanwhile, place jelly in medium microwavable bowl and heat in microwave on **HIGH** 10 seconds. Stir in apple, celery, carrot, raisins and lemon juice. Serve salsa with pita chips.

Makes 3 servings

Banana Caterpillars

2 medium bananas
¼ cup peanut butter
¼ cup flaked coconut
4 raisins
6 thin pretzel sticks

1. Peel and cut each banana into 10 slices. Assemble "caterpillar" by spreading slices with peanut butter and pressing pieces together.

2. Sprinkle half of coconut over each "caterpillar" and press lightly with fingertips to coat. Use additional peanut butter to press raisins on one end to form "eyes." Break pretzel sticks into small pieces and press between banana slices for "legs" and "antennae."

Makes 2 servings

•super suggestion • • • • • • • • • • • • • • • • •

Kids can also be creative and add other types of sliced fruits (strawberries, apples, pears) to their caterpillars.

Maraschino-Lemonade Pops

1 (10-ounce) jar
   maraschino cherries
8 (3-ounce) paper cups
1 (12-ounce) can frozen
   pink lemonade
   concentrate, partly
   thawed
¼ cup water
8 popsicle sticks

Drain cherries, reserving juice. Place one whole cherry in each paper cup. Coarsely chop remaining cherries. Add chopped cherries, lemonade concentrate, water and reserved juice to container of blender or food processor; blend until smooth. Fill paper cups with equal amounts of cherry mixture. Freeze several hours or until very slushy. Place popsicle sticks in the center of each cup. Freeze 1 hour longer or until firm. To serve, peel off paper cups.

Makes 8 servings

Note: Serve immediately after peeling off paper cups—these pops melt very quickly.

Favorite recipe from *Cherry Marketing Institute*

Mysterious Colorful Jiggles

1 package (4-serving size) lime gelatin or flavor of your choice
1 package (4-serving size) orange gelatin or flavor of your choice
1 package (4-serving size) blue raspberry gelatin or flavor of your choice
Whipped topping
Colored sprinkles

1. Prepare lime gelatin according to package directions and place in small pitcher or 2-cup measuring cup. Pour ¼ cup lime gelatin mixture into each of 8 (8- to 10-ounce) clear plastic cups. Refrigerate 2 hours or until gelatin is firm.

2. Meanwhile, prepare orange gelatin according to package directions and place in small pitcher or 2-cup measuring cup. Refrigerate 1 hour or until gelatin just begins to gel.

3. Remove lime gelatin cups from refrigerator. Pour ¼ cup orange gelatin into cups and refrigerate until firm; about 2 hours.

4. Meanwhile, prepare blue raspberry gelatin according to package directions and place in small pitcher or 2-cup measuring cup. Refrigerate 1 hour or until gelatin just begins to gel.

5. Remove gelatin cups from refrigerator. Pour ¼ cup blue raspberry gelatin into cups and refrigerate until firm; about 2 hours.

6. Serve with whipped topping and sprinkles. *Makes 8 servings*

Cherry Tomato Pops

4 (1-ounce) part-skim
    mozzarella cheese
    sticks
8 cherry tomatoes
3 tablespoons fat-free ranch
    dressing

1. Slice cheese sticks in half lengthwise. Trim stem end of each cherry tomato and remove pulp and seeds.

2. Press end of cheese stick into hollowed tomato to make Cherry Tomato Pop. Serve with ranch dressing for dipping.

Makes 8 pops

super suggestion

Try dipping these crazy pops in thousand island, French or salsa ranch dressings.

CHERRY TOMATO POPS

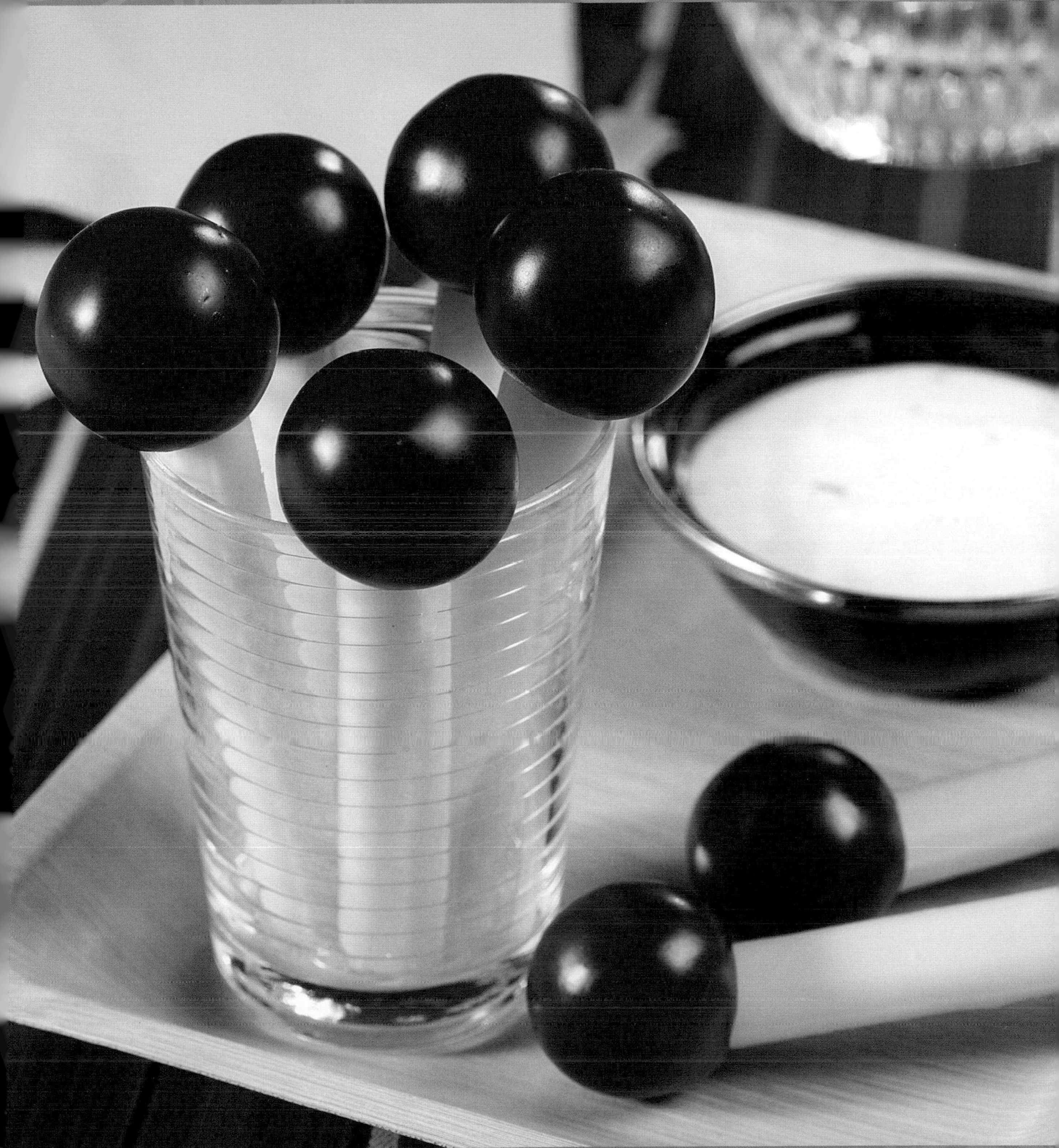

Cinnamon Apple Chips

2 cups unsweetened apple
    juice
1 cinnamon stick
2 Washington Red
    Delicious apples

1. In large skillet or saucepan, combine apple juice and cinnamon stick; bring to a low boil while preparing apples.

2. With paring knife, slice off ½ inch from tops and bottoms of apples and discard (or eat). Stand apples on either cut end; cut crosswise into ⅛-inch-thick slices, rotating apple as necessary to cut even slices.

3. Drop slices into boiling juice; cook 4 to 5 minutes or until slices appear translucent and lightly golden. Meanwhile, preheat oven to 250°F.

4. With slotted spatula, remove apple slices from juice and pat dry. Arrange slices on wire racks, making sure none overlap. Place racks on middle shelf in oven; bake 30 to 40 minutes until slices are lightly browned and almost dry to touch. Let chips cool on racks completely before storing in airtight container.

Makes about 40 chips

Tip: There is no need to core apples because boiling in juice for several minutes softens core and removes seeds.

Favorite recipe from ***Washington Apple Commission***

CINNAMON APPLE CHIPS

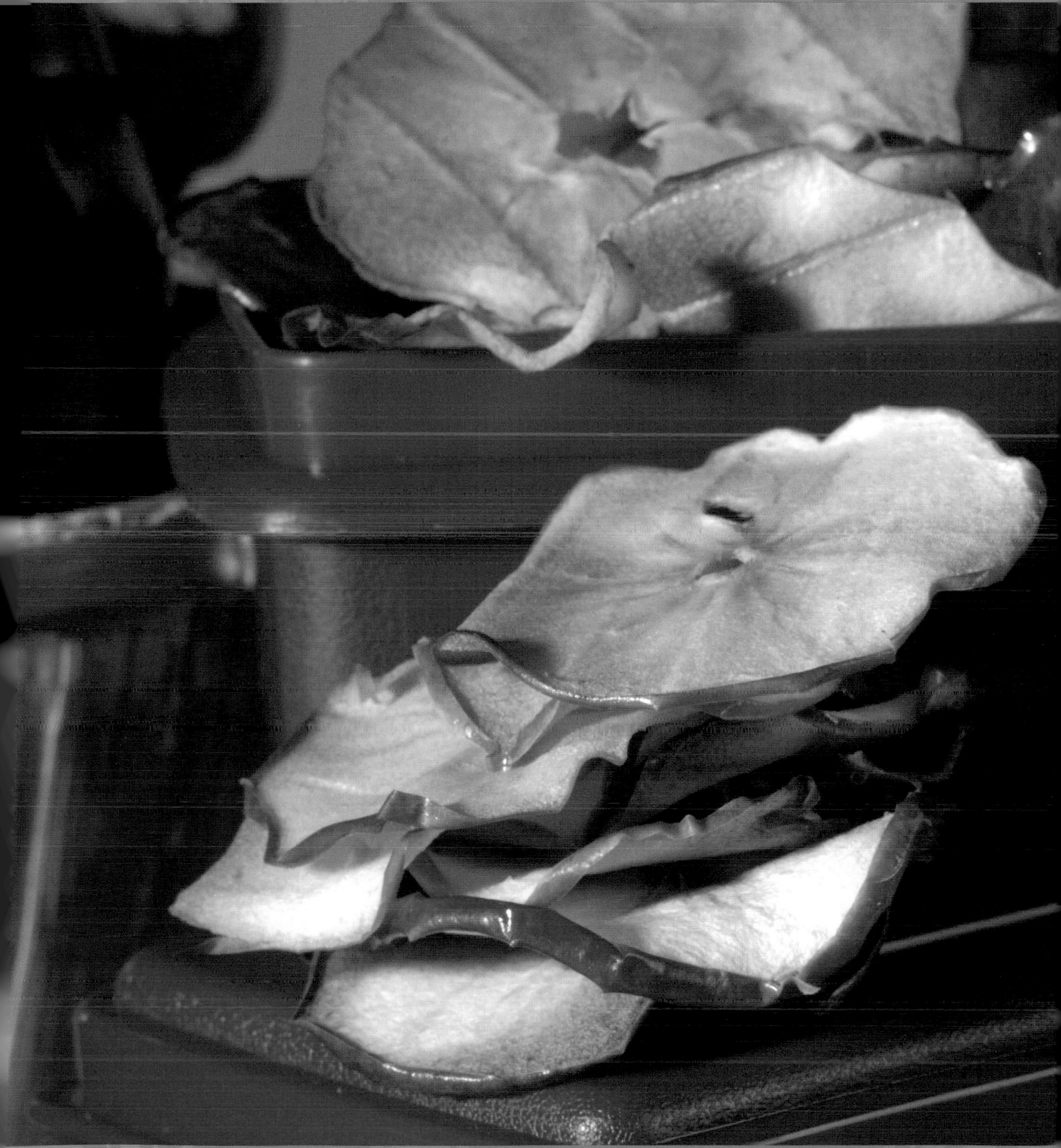

Peachy Pops

Prep Time: 20 minutes • **Freeze Time:** 4 hours

1 package (16 ounces)
   frozen sliced peaches,
   softened not thawed
2 containers (8 ounces
   each) peach or vanilla
   yogurt
¼ cup honey
12 popsicle sticks or lollipop
   sticks
12 small paper cups
   Sugar sprinkles

1. Place peaches, yogurt and honey in food processor or blender. Cover and process until mixture is fairly smooth, about 20 seconds, scraping down sides as needed.

2. Pour peach mixture into paper cups and place on baking sheet. Freeze peach mixture 1 hour or until mixture begins to harden. Push popsicle sticks into centers and freeze an additional 3 hours or until firm. Tear paper away from pops and roll in sugar sprinkles. Serve immediately or return to freezer until serving time.

Makes 12 (½ cup) servings

Secret Ingredient Brownies

Prep Time: 15 minutes • **Bake Time:** 30 minutes

1 cup packed brown sugar
1 cup applesauce
½ cup (1 stick) butter or margarine, melted
2 eggs
1 teaspoon vanilla
1 cup all-purpose flour
⅓ cup unsweetened cocoa powder
⅓ cup mini chocolate chips
2 teaspoons baking powder
2 teaspoons baking soda
½ teaspoon salt
½ teaspoon ground cinnamon
⅓ cup powdered sugar

1. Preheat oven to 350°F. Spray 8-inch square pan with nonstick cooking spray. Whisk together brown sugar, applesauce, butter, eggs and vanilla in large bowl until well blended. Stir in flour, cocoa powder, chocolate chips, baking powder, baking soda, salt and cinnamon; mix well.

2. Pour batter into prepared pan. Bake 30 to 35 minutes or until sides shrink away slightly from sides of pan and toothpick inserted into center comes out clean. Cool in pan on wire rack. Dust with powdered sugar just before serving. Cut into squares to serve.

Makes 16 brownies

Note: Brownies will stay fresh up to 3 days. Simply wrap and store and room temperature.

Banana S'mores

Prep Time: 5 minutes • **Cook Time:** 1 minute

1 firm DOLE® Banana, sliced
12 graham cracker squares
6 large marshmallows
1 bar (1.55 ounces) milk chocolate candy

MICROWAVE DIRECTIONS

• Arrange 4 banana slices on each of 6 graham cracker squares. Top with marshmallow. Microwave on HIGH 12 to 15 seconds or until puffed.

• Place 2 squares chocolate on remaining 6 graham crackers. Microwave on HIGH 1 minute or until just soft. Put halves together to make sandwich.

Makes 6 servings

Orange You Glad Dessert

Prep Time: 20 minutes • **Freeze Time:** 5 hours

1. Carefully cut pulp from oranges with small knife and spoon. Place pulp in blender container. Reserve empty orange shells.

2. Process pulp, yogurt, orange juice concentrate, vanilla and food coloring, if desired, in blender until almost smooth, about 12 seconds.

3. Spoon orange mixture into 4 reserved orange halves, mounding mixture on top. Cover loosely with plastic wrap and freeze until firm, about 4 hours. Remove plastic wrap. Place remaining orange halves on top of orange mixture. Place oranges in freezer-safe bowls; freeze at least 1 hour before serving. Garnish with mint leaves, if desired.

Makes 4 servings

4 naval oranges, halved
3 containers (8 ounces each) orange, lemon or vanilla yogurt
2 tablespoons frozen orange juice concentrate
1 teaspoon vanilla
  Red food coloring (optional)
4 mint leaves (optional)

Funny Face Pizza Snacks

Preheat oven to 350°F.

Lightly toast English muffins in toaster. Arrange on a baking sheet and spread each muffin with sauce, then top with cheese. Cut vegetables and meat into shapes as suggested below. Bake for 12 to 15 minutes or until cheese melts.

Makes 8 servings

4 English muffins, split
½ cup pizza sauce or low-fat pasta sauce
¾ cup part-skim shredded mozzarella cheese
  Vegetables and ham or pepperoni

Suggestions for faces: Eyes: olives, mushrooms or carrot strips. Nose: cherry tomato half, zucchini slice, mushroom, pepperoni or ham. Mouth: bell pepper slices or carrot strips. Hair: strips of ham, cauliflower or broccoli florets cut in small pieces.

Favorite recipe from **Wheat Foods Council**

Banana Split Shakes

1 small (6-inch) ripe
   banana
¼ cup fat-free (skim) milk
5 maraschino cherries,
   drained
1 tablespoon light
   chocolate syrup
⅛ teaspoon coconut extract
4 cups low-fat chocolate
   frozen yogurt

1. Combine banana, milk, cherries, chocolate syrup and coconut extract in blender. Cover; blend on HIGH speed until smooth.

2. Add frozen yogurt 1 cup at a time. Cover and pulse on HIGH speed after each addition until smooth and thick. Pour into 4 glasses. Garnish with additional maraschino cherries, if desired.

Makes 4 servings

Tip: For an even healthier shake, chop 3 large, peeled bananas. Place in resealable plastic bag and freeze until solid. (This is a great use for over-ripe bananas). Blend with milk, cherries, chocolate syrup and coconut extract. It will not be as thick and frosty, but will be lower in calories and fat.

Red Hot Apple Mug

Prep Time: 5 minutes

4 teaspoons red cinnamon
candies
1 quart apple juice
½ teaspoon cinnamon or
peppermint extract
(optional)
4 candy cinnamon or
peppermint sticks
(5 inches each)

1. Place 1 teaspoon cinnamon candies in each of 4 mugs. Heat apple juice and cinnamon extract, if desired, in medium saucepan over medium heat until hot but not boiling.

2. Pour hot apple juice into mugs and add candy cinnamon stick for stirring.

Makes 4 servings

super suggestion

Candies will dissolve into apple juice completely after about 10 minutes and color the juice red.

RED HOT APPLE MUG

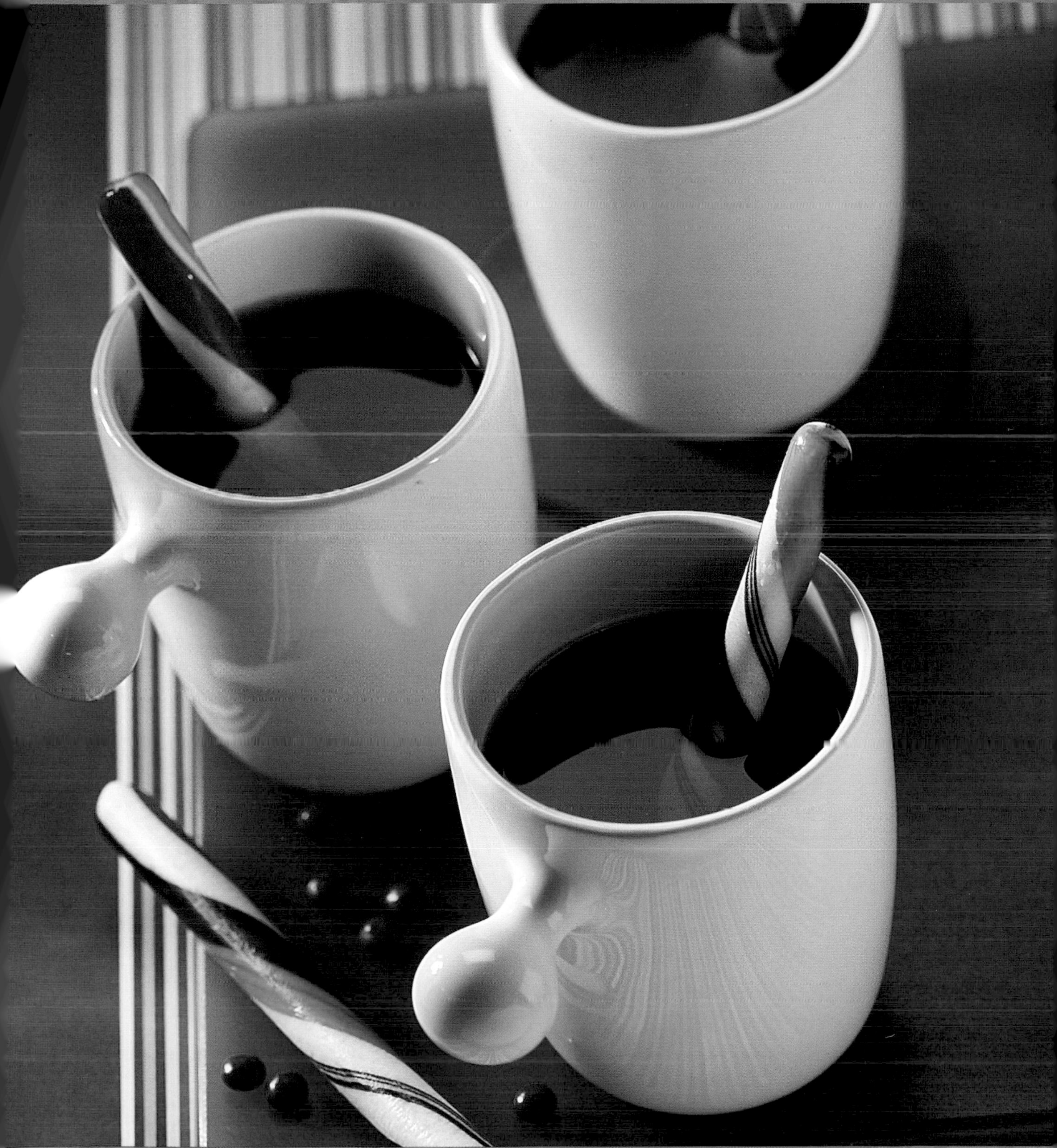

Chilling Out Watermelon Soda

Prep Time: 10 minutes

¾ cup frozen orange-
  pineapple-apple juice
  concentrate, thawed
6 cups cubed seeded
  watermelon
2 cups sparkling water or
  club soda
  Ice cubes
6 small watermelon wedges

1. Combine concentrate and watermelon in blender or food processor. Cover and process until smooth. Divide water and ice cubes among 6 (8-ounce) glasses. Pour watermelon mixture over water in glasses. Stir to combine.

2. Garnish each with watermelon wedge.

Makes 6 (8-ounce) servings

Mysterious Chocolate Mint Cooler

2 cups cold whole milk or
  half-and-half
¼ cup chocolate syrup
1 teaspoon peppermint
  extract
  Crushed ice
  Aerosol whipped topping
  Mint leaves

Combine milk, chocolate syrup and peppermint extract in small pitcher; stir until well blended. Fill 2 glasses with crushed ice. Pour chocolate-mint mixture over ice. Top with whipped topping. Garnish with mint leaves.

Makes about 2 (10-ounce) servings

CHILLING OUT WATERMELON SODA

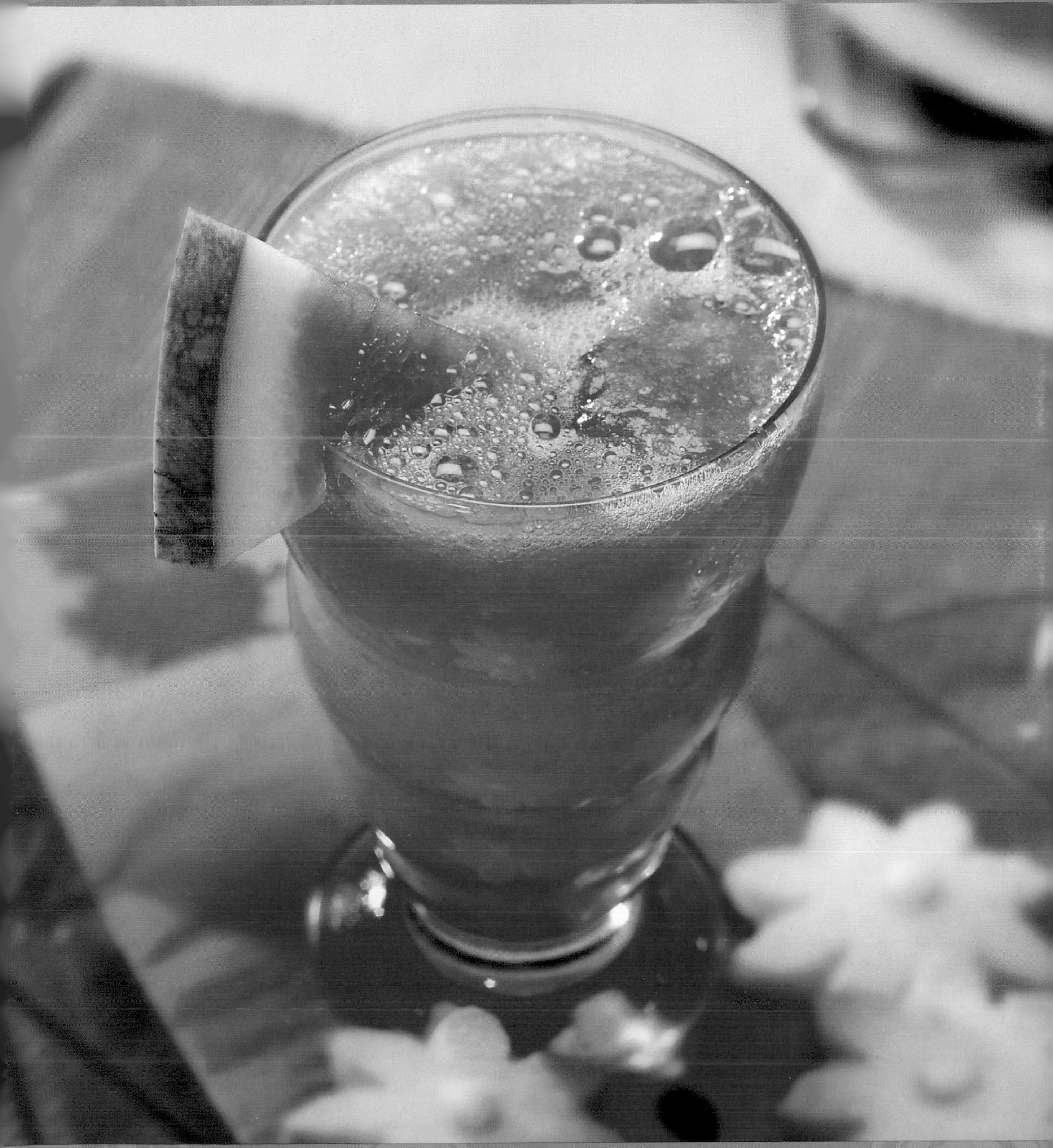

Frozen Florida Monkey Malts

Prep Time: 5 minutes

2 bananas, peeled
1 cup milk
5 tablespoons frozen orange juice concentrate
3 tablespoons malted milk powder

1. Wrap bananas in plastic wrap; freeze.

2. Break bananas into pieces; place in blender with milk, orange juice concentrate and malted milk powder. Blend until smooth; pour into glasses to serve.

Makes 2 servings

Creamy Crypt Coolers

2 cups orange sherbet
2 cups vanilla ice cream
2 cups orange juice
5 drops yellow food coloring
5 drops red food coloring
1 cup lemon-lime soda

1. Combine sherbet, ice cream, juice and food colorings in blender. Process until smooth.

2. Add soda. Hold lid down tightly and process until just blended. Serve immediately.

Makes 5 cups

super suggestion

Serve in creepy, Halloween-themed cups with spooky straws.

Apricot Peachy Chiller

1 can (about 9 ounces) apricots in heavy syrup

1 cup cut-up frozen peach slices

½ cup frozen whole unsweetened strawberries

1 container (6 ounces) vanilla yogurt

1 to 2 tablespoons fresh lemon juice (optional)

Place all ingredients in blender. Cover; process 15 to 30 seconds until smooth, using on/off pulsing action to break up chunks. Divide between glasses; serve immediately.

Makes 4 (³/₄-cup) servings

Soy Apricot Peachy Chiller: Substitute 1 container (6 ounces) vanilla or peach soy yogurt for the regular vanilla yogurt.

Cookie Milk Shakes

1 pint vanilla ice cream

4 chocolate sandwich cookies or chocolate-covered graham crackers

1. Scoop ice cream into blender. Crush cookies in resealable food storage bag with rolling pin or in food processor.

2. Place cookies in blender. Process until well combined. Pour into 2 glasses. Serve immediately. *Makes 2 servings*

Frozen Apple Slushies

1 large (about 10 ounces)
   Red Delicious apple,
   peeled and cut into
   chunks
1 cup 100% cranberry
   juice, chilled
½ cup frozen unsweetened
   apple juice concentrate
⅛ teaspoon ground
   cinnamon
3 cups ice cubes

Place apple chunks, cranberry juice, concentrate and cinnamon in blender; cover and process until smooth. Add ice cubes, 1 cup at a time; cover and process after each addition until smooth and icy. Serve with straw or spoon.

Makes 4 servings

super suggestion

Freeze leftovers in 1-cup servings in small airtight microwavable containers. To serve, microwave each serving for 15 seconds on HIGH; stir. Continue microwaving in 10-second increments until slushy.

Cherry Chocolate Frosty

1 container (6 ounces) chocolate yogurt
½ cup frozen dark sweet cherries
⅛ to ¼ teaspoon almond extract

1. Combine all ingredients in blender container. Cover; blend on high speed 15 to 30 seconds until smooth.

2. Pour into glass; serve immediately.

Makes 1 (¾-cup) serving

Sparkling Strawberry Float

Prep Time: 10 minutes

2 tablespoons pink decorative sugar (optional)
2 cups (8 ounces) frozen unsweetened strawberries
1 container (6 ounces) strawberry yogurt
½ cup milk
2 tablespoons honey or sugar
2 scoops strawberry sorbet
2 fresh strawberries (optional)

1. Place sugar in small shallow dish. Wet rims of glasses with damp paper towel; dip into sugar. Place glasses upright to dry.

2. Place frozen strawberries, yogurt, milk and honey in blender; process until smooth. Divide between prepared glasses. Top each glass with scoop of strawberry sorbet. If desired, cut fresh strawberries from tip almost to stem end; place on rim of glasses.

Makes 2 servings

Jungle Juice

1 banana
1 cup frozen strawberries
1 container (6 ounces)
    vanilla low-fat yogurt
2 tablespoons frozen
    orange juice
    concentrate
2 tablespoons strawberry
    syrup
  Fresh orange slices
    (optional)

1. Place banana, strawberries, yogurt and concentrate in blender. Process until smooth, scraping down sides of blender as needed.

2. Evenly drizzle syrup around inside of 2 tall, clear glasses. Pour Jungle Juice into glasses. Garnish with orange slices, if desired.

Makes 2 servings

Maraschino Cherry Shake

1 (10-ounce) jar
    maraschino cherries
3 tablespoons maraschino
    cherry juice
3 cups vanilla ice cream
  Whipped topping
  Whole maraschino
    cherries, for garnish

Put a colander or strainer in a bowl. Pour cherries into the strainer. Measure out 3 tablespoons of juice and put it in a small container. You will use these 3 tablespoons of juice to prepare this recipe. You can either discard the remaining juice or save it for another use.

Put cherries from the strainer on a cutting board. With a knife, carefully cut cherries into small pieces. Have an adult show you how to use the knife.

Put chopped cherries, 3 tablespoons juice and ice cream in the container of an electric blender or food processor; cover. Process or blend until smooth. Do not put a spoon or spatula in the blender while it is running and keep your hands clear of the working parts.

Pour into 2 (12-ounce) glasses. Top with whipped topping; garnish with whole maraschino cherries.

Makes 2 (12-ounce) servings

Favorite recipe from ***Cherry Marketing Institute***

Putrid Bug Potion

3 cups lime sherbet
1 cup pineapple juice
1 package (.13-ounce)
   grape-flavored
   drink mix
2 cups ginger ale
   Frozen seedless red
   grapes (optional)

1. Combine sherbet, juice and drink mix in blender. Process until smooth.

2. Add ginger ale. Cover; process until just blended.

3. Add frozen grapes, if desired. Serve immediately.

Makes 5 cups

Tip: Fake ice cubes with bugs or other critters can be added for an extra-buggy presentation. Make this grayish, ghoulish concoction pale pink by substituting cherry-flavor drink mix for the grape.

Black Forest Smoothie

1 container (6 ounces) dark
   cherry-flavored yogurt
½ cup frozen dark sweet
   cherries
¼ cup milk
2 tablespoons sugar
2 tablespoons cocoa
¼ teaspoon almond extract
1 to 2 ice cubes

Place all ingredients in blender. Cover; process 15 to 30 seconds until smooth, using on/off pulsing action to break up chunks. Divide between 2 glasses and serve. *Makes 2 (¾-cup) servings*

PUTRID BUG POTION

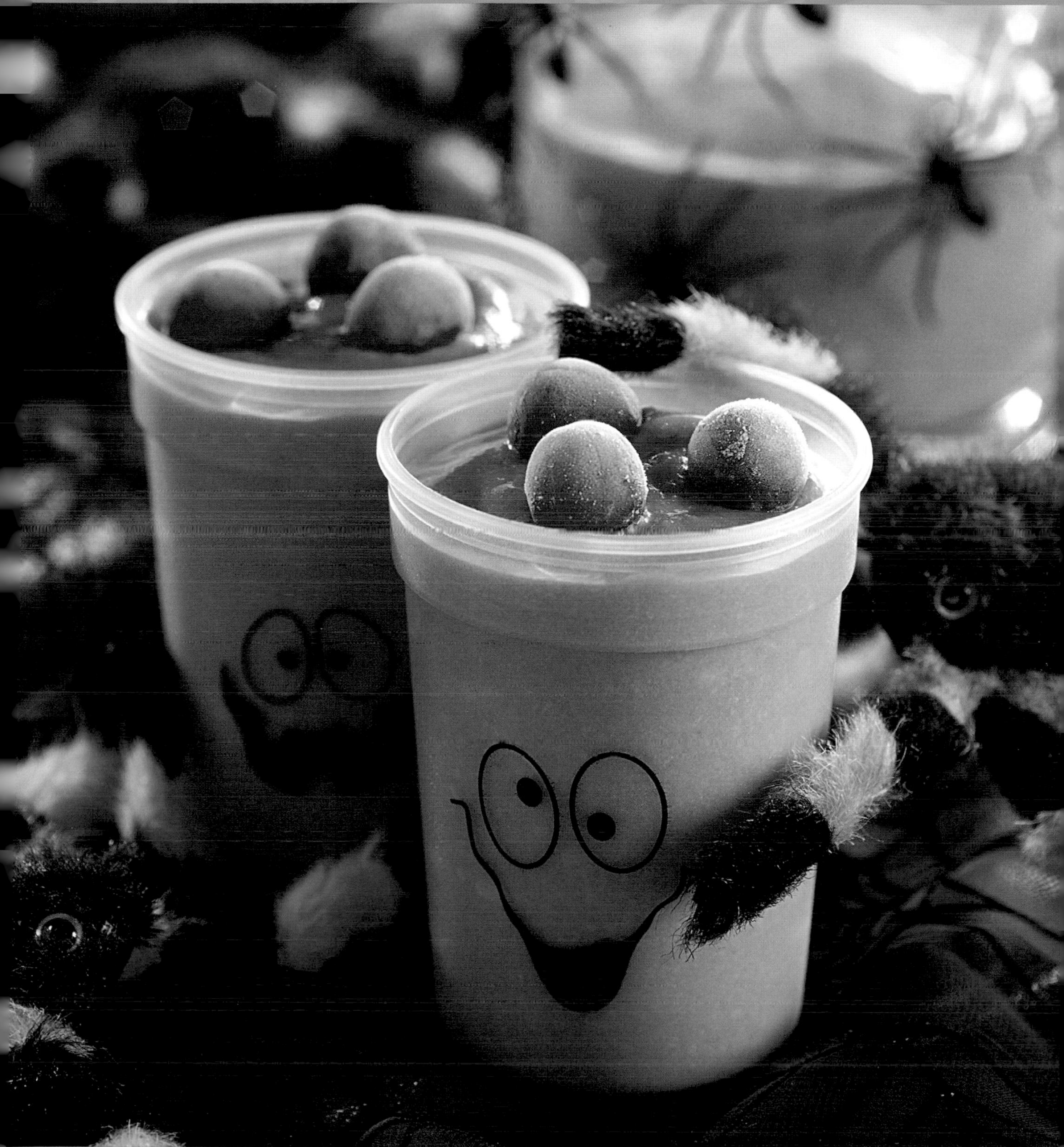

Tofu Orange Dream

½ cup soft tofu
½ cup orange juice
1 container (about
    2½ ounces) baby
    food carrots
2 tablespoons honey *or*
    1 tablespoon sugar
¼ teaspoon fresh grated
    ginger
2 to 3 ice cubes

Place all ingredients in blender. Cover; process 15 seconds until smooth. Pour into glass; serve immediately.

Makes 1 (1-cup) serving

Kiwi Strawberry Smoothie

2 kiwi, peeled and sliced
1 cup frozen whole
    unsweetened
    strawberries
1 container (6 ounces)
    strawberry yogurt
½ cup milk
2 tablespoons honey

Place all ingredients in blender. Cover; process 15 to 30 seconds until smooth, using on/off pulsing action to break up chunks. Divide between 2 glasses and serve.　*Makes 2 (1-cup) servings*

Soy Kiwi Strawberry Smoothie: Substitute 1 container (6 ounces) strawberry soy yogurt for regular strawberry yogurt.

Banana Roll-Ups

¼ cup smooth or crunchy
   almond butter
2 tablespoons mini
   chocolate chips
1 to 2 tablespoons milk
1 (8-inch) whole wheat
   flour tortilla
1 large banana, peeled

1. Combine almond butter, chocolate chips and 1 tablespoon milk in medium microwavable bowl. Microwave on MEDIUM (50%) 40 seconds. Stir well and repeat, if necessary, to melt chocolate. Add more milk, if necessary, for desired consistency.

2. Spread almond butter mixture on tortilla. Place banana on one side of tortilla and roll up tightly. Cut into 8 slices.

Makes 4 servings

Chocolate Chip Cannoli Cones

Prep Time: 25 minutes

1¼ cup mini chocolate chips, divided
1 teaspoon canola oil
10 sugar ice cream cones
1 container (15 ounces) whole milk or part-skim ricotta cheese
⅔ cup powdered sugar
½ cup thawed frozen reduced-fat whipped topping
2 tablespoons peach or orange marmalade
10 maraschino cherries

1. Place 1 cup mini chocolate chips and oil in shallow dish and microwave 10 seconds. Stir; repeat until chips are melted. Dip edge of each cone into melted chocolate; place on waxed paper to harden. Place cones in refrigerator to harden quickly, if desired.

2. Combine 2 tablespoons chocolate chips, ricotta cheese, powdered sugar, whipped topping and marmalade in medium bowl. (Mixture can be covered and refrigerated until serving time, up to 24 hours.) Spoon mixture into chocolate-dipped cones. Sprinkle remaining 2 tablespoons chocolate chips over top and place one cherry in center of each cone. Serve immediately.

Makes 10 servings

•super suggestion

These silly treats can be made for adults too. After dipping cones in melted chocolate, sprinkle with chopped pistachio nuts. Use orange marmalade instead of peach marmalade in cannoli mixture. Omit cherry and sprinkle with additional pistachio nuts.

Cracker Toffee

72 rectangular butter-
    flavored crackers
1 cup (2 sticks) unsalted
    butter
1 cup packed brown sugar
¼ teaspoon salt
2½ cups semisweet chocolate
    chips
2 cups chopped pecans

1. Preheat oven to 375°F. Line 17×12-inch jelly-roll pan with heavy-duty foil. Spray generously with nonstick cooking spray. Arrange crackers with edges touching in pan; set aside.

2. Combine butter, brown sugar and salt in heavy medium saucepan. Heat over medium heat until butter melts, stirring frequently. Increase heat to high; boil 3 minutes without stirring. Pour mixture evenly over crackers; spread to cover.

3. Bake 5 minutes. Immediately sprinkle chocolate chips evenly over crackers; spread to cover. Sprinkle pecans over chocolate, pressing down. Cool to room temperature. Refrigerate 2 hours. Break into chunks to serve. *Makes 24 servings*

Variation: Substitute peanut butter chips for chocolate chips and coarsely chopped, lightly salted peanuts for chopped pecans.

Gooey Coconut Chocolate Cupcakes

1 box (18 ounces)
   chocolate cake mix,
   plus ingredients to
   prepare mix
½ cup (1 stick) butter or
   margarine
1 cup packed brown sugar
⅓ cup cream, half-and-half
   or milk
1½ cups sweetened flaked
   coconut
½ cup chopped pecans
   (optional)

1. Preheat oven to 350°F. Line 24 standard (2½-inch) muffin cups with foil baking cups. Prepare cake mix according to package directions. Pour batter into prepared muffin cups, filling each cup about half full. Bake 18 minutes or until toothpick inserted into centers comes out clean. Do not remove cupcakes from pan. Preheat broiler.

2. Meanwhile, melt butter in a medium saucepan over low heat. Stir in brown sugar and cream until well blended and sugar is dissolved. Add coconut and pecans, if desired, and mix well.

3. Spread 2 to 3 tablespoons frosting over each cupcake. Place cupcakes under broiler 2 to 3 minutes or until tops begin to brown and bubble around the edges. Serve warm or cool.

Makes 24 cupcakes

Leapin' Lizards!

1. Line baking sheet with waxed paper.

2. Combine butterscotch chips, corn syrup and butter in large saucepan. Stir over medium heat until chips are melted. Add white chocolate chips and green food coloring; stir well. Remove from heat. Add cereal; stir to coat evenly.

3. Lightly butter hands and shape about 1½ cups cereal mixture into lizard (about 6 inches long). Place on prepared baking sheet. Decorate with candies. Repeat with remaining mixture.

Makes 4 lizards

1 cup butterscotch baking chips
½ cup corn syrup
3 tablespoons butter
1 cup white chocolate chips
Green food coloring
7 cups crisp rice cereal
Candy corn, green jelly beans, red miniature jaw breakers and chocolate chips

Meteorite Mini Cakes

1 package (18¼ ounces)
chocolate cake mix,
plus ingredients to
prepare mix
2 containers (16 ounces
each) vanilla frosting,
divided
Assorted food coloring
1 bag (11 ounces)
chocolate baking
chunks

1. Preheat oven to 350°F. Spray 12 standard (2½-inch) muffin cups with nonstick cooking spray. Prepare cake mix according to package directions. Divide batter evenly among muffin cups. Bake 20 to 25 minutes or until toothpick inserted into centers comes out clean. Cool 5 minutes on wire rack; remove from pan and cool completely.

2. Use kitchen shears to trim cupcake edges and form rounded, irregular shapes. Place 2 cups frosting in microwavable bowl and heat on LOW (30%), until melted, about 30 seconds. Tint as desired with food coloring. Stir until smooth. Drizzle frosting over cupcakes, coating completely.

3. Chill cakes 20 minutes. Dot cakes with chocolate baking chunks to make meteorite surface. Melt and tint remaining frosting as desired and coat baking chunks with frosting. Chill until ready to serve.

Makes 12 servings

Mud Hole Dunk

Prep Time: 20 minutes

4 cups fresh strawberries, cut-up fresh pineapple and seedless grapes

1 cup prepared creamy chocolate frosting*

Assorted decorator sprinkles or flaked coconut

Do not use whipped frosting.

1. Line baking sheet with waxed paper. Set aside. Pat fruit dry with paper towels.

2. Microwave frosting on HIGH 15 to 20 seconds or until melted, stirring once.

3. Dip fruit halfway into frosting, allowing excess to drip off. Roll in sprinkles or coconut. Place on prepared baking sheet. Refrigerate about 10 minutes or until frosting is set.

Makes 8 servings

super suggestion

To make this tasty recipe even easier, look for already cut-up fruit at your supermarket salad bar.

Popcorn Truffles

8 cups popped plain
   popcorn
2 cups (12 ounces)
   semisweet chocolate
   chips
Colored sprinkles
   (optional)

1. Line 2 baking sheets with waxed paper. Place popcorn in large bowl.

2. Place chocolate chips in microwavable bowl. Microwave on HIGH 30 seconds; stir. Repeat, if necessary, until chips are melted. Pour over popcorn; stir until well coated.

3. Scoop popcorn mixture with small ice cream scoop, pressing mixture slightly against the inside of bowl. Drop by scoopfuls onto prepared baking sheets. Decorate with sprinkles, if desired. Allow to harden at room temperature or refrigerate. Store truffles in airtight container up to 3 days. *Makes 40 (1½-inch) truffles*

Pretty Pink Pies

Prep Time: 10 minutes

1 small ripe banana, sliced

1 package (4 ounces) mini graham cracker crumb pie crusts (6 crusts)

2 tablespoons chocolate ice cream topping

2 containers (6 ounces each) strawberry low-fat yogurt

6 mini pastel marshmallows or mini marshmallows

6 medium fresh strawberries, cut into wedges

1. Divide banana slices between pie crusts. Drizzle each with 1 teaspoon chocolate topping. Spoon yogurt over top.

2. Place 1 marshmallow in the center of each tart. Arrange strawberry wedges around marshmallow to resemble flower. Serve immediately or cover and refrigerate up to 4 hours.

Makes 6 servings

super suggestion

Make one big delicious pie instead of the mini ones. Use a 6-ounce prepared graham cracker crust in place of mini crusts. Follow directions as above, place all ingredients in large crust.

Pretzel Fried Eggs

24 (1-inch) pretzel rings
1 cup white chocolate
    chips
24 yellow candy-coated
    chocolate pieces

1. Line baking sheet with waxed paper. Place pretzel rings on prepared baking sheet about 2 inches apart.

2. Place white chocolate chips in 1-quart resealable food storage bag; seal bag. Microwave on HIGH 30 seconds. Knead bag gently and microwave 30 seconds more; repeat until chips are melted. Cut ¼-inch corner from bag.

3. Squeeze chocolate from bag onto each pretzel ring in circular motion. Fill center of pretzel first and finish with ring of chocolate around edge of pretzel. Use tip of small knife to smooth chocolate, if necessary. Place candy piece in center of each pretzel. Allow to harden at room temperature or refrigerate until set. Store in single layer in airtight container up to one week. *Makes 24 eggs*

Variation: To make "green eggs and ham," use green candy-coated chocolate pieces for "yolks." Cut small pieces of pink fruit leather for "ham." Serve 2 Pretzel Fried Eggs with "ham" and square cinnamon cereal for "toast."

Reese's® Peanut Butter and Milk Chocolate Chip Cattails

1 cup HERSHEY'S® Milk
    Chocolate Chips,
    divided
1 cup REESE'S® Peanut
    Butter Chips, divided
2 teaspoons shortening
    (do not use butter,
    margarine, spread
    or oil)
12 to 14 pretzel rods

1. Stir together milk chocolate chips and peanut butter chips. Place sheet of wax paper on tray or counter top. Finely chop 1 cup chip mixture in food processor or by hand; place on wax paper. Line tray or cookie sheet with wax paper.

2. Place remaining 1 cup chip mixture and shortening in narrow deep microwave-safe bowl. Microwave at MEDIUM (50%) 1 minute; stir. If necessary, microwave additional 30 seconds at a time, stirring after each heating, until chips are melted and mixture is smooth when stirred.

3. Spoon chocolate-peanut butter mixture over about three fourths of pretzel rod; gently shake off excess. Holding pretzel by uncoated end roll in chopped chips, pressing chips into chocolate. Place on prepared tray. Refrigerate 30 minutes or until set. Store coated pretzels in cool, dry place. *Makes 12 to 14 coated pretzels*

Variation: Melt entire package of chips with 4 teaspoons shortening and dip small pretzels into mixture.

Mice Creams

Prep Time: 15 minutes

Place 1 scoop vanilla ice cream into each crust. Press cookie ears and tails into ice cream. Press eyes, noses and whiskers into place. Serve immediately. Do not refreeze.   *Makes 6 servings*

•super suggestion •••••••••••••••••••

For variety, experiment with this recipe by using your child's favorite ice cream flavors. Try chocolate, chocolate chip or even mint chocolate chip.

1 pint vanilla ice cream
1 (4-ounce) package READY CRUST® Mini-Graham Cracker Pie Crusts
Ears—12 KEEBLER® Grasshopper® cookies
Tails—3 chocolate twigs, broken in half *or* 6 (3-inch) pieces black shoestring licorice
Eyes and noses— 18 brown candy-coated chocolate candies
Whiskers—2 teaspoons chocolate sprinkles

Acknowledgments

The publisher would like to thank the companies and organizations listed below for the use of their recipes and photographs in this publication.

Cherry Marketing Institute

Chilean Fresh Fruit Association

Dole Food Company, Inc.

The Hershey Company

Hostess®

Keebler® Company

© Mars, Incorporated 2007

Reckitt Benckiser Inc.

Unilever

Veg•All®

Washington Apple Commission

Wheat Foods Council

Index